SOMETIMES
I THINK
ABOUT IT

Also by Stephen Elliott

Novels

Happy Baby
What It Means to Love You
A Life Without Consequences
Jones Inn

Erotica

My Girlfriend Comes to the City and Beats Me Up

Nonfiction

The Adderall Diaries
*Looking Forward to It: Or, How I Learned to Stop
Worrying and Love the American Electoral Process*

As Editor

Where to Invade Next
Sex for America
Stumbling and Raging: More Politically Inspired Fiction
Politically Inspired: Fiction for Our Time

Co-writer with Eric Martin

Donald

SOMETIMES I THINK ABOUT IT

ESSAYS

STEPHEN ELLIOTT

GRAYWOLF PRESS

Some of the essays in this collection appeared originally in different form in the following publications:

"Where I Slept," "An Interview with My Father," and "An Interview with Lorelei Lee" in the *Rumpus*, "My Little Brother Ruined My Life" in *Maisonneuve*, "Hate To Be Alone" in *McSweeney's*, "Sometimes I Think About Suicide" in the *Sun*, "Jimmy Wallet Is Buried Alive" in *Esquire*, "The New New Middle East" and "The Score" in the *Believer*, "California Superpredator" in *LA Weekly*, "Why Britney Matters" in the *Stranger*, "The DIY Book Tour" in the *New York Times Book Review*, and "Silicon Is Just Sand" in *Epic Magazine*.

This publication is made possible, in part, by the voters of Minnesota through a Minnesota State Arts Board Operating Support grant, thanks to a legislative appropriation from the arts and cultural heritage fund, and a grant from the Wells Fargo Foundation. Significant support has also been provided by Target, the McKnight Foundation, the Lannan Foundation, the Amazon Literary Partnership, and other generous contributions from foundations, corporations, and individuals. To these organizations and individuals we offer our heartfelt thanks.

Published by Graywolf Press
250 Third Avenue North, Suite 600
Minneapolis, Minnesota 55401

www.graywolfpress.org

Published in the United States of America

ISBN 978-1-55597-775-7

2 4 6 8 9 7 5 3 1
First Graywolf Printing, 2017

Library of Congress Control Number: 2017930119

Cover design: Steve Attardo

Cover art: Shutterstock

It is impossible to forgive whoever has done us harm if that harm has lowered us. We have to think that it has not lowered us but revealed to us our true level. —Simone Weil

Contents

These essays were written between 2003 and 2015. They're mostly personal essays. After assembling them, I went through, pulling out redundancies. Sometimes the echoes were interesting, and I let them remain. Sometimes I didn't feel that an essay represented me anymore but decided to keep it anyway. That's the problem with writing things down; we change, the person who wrote is no longer there.

SOMETIMES
I THINK
ABOUT IT

In Country

"What are you thinking?" she asked, climbing next to me in the bed, still fully dressed.

Where I Slept

My homeless year began early in October 1985 and ended the last day of August 1986. I was thirteen, and then fourteen, and it's a story I've never told, partly because I slept in so many places that year. I slept in the broom closet of a friend's apartment building. The closet was just inside the entryway, past the eight slotted mailboxes. It was the size of a single bed, crowded with mop buckets and cleaning solutions, and I could stretch all the way out and my toes would just touch the door. The building itself was a tan brick four-flat. Kwan lived with his parents and grandmother in a two-bedroom on the second floor, part of a wave of Korean immigrants who had arrived on the North Side of Chicago in the early eighties, on their way to the suburbs, along with the Kurds and Russian Jews. When I would come over to visit after school, Kwan's grandmother would clutch my head in her bony hands and pray for me.

"She wants to know if you're going to church," Kwan would explain. When it was time for dinner, Kwan would politely ask me to leave.

I had a leather bomber jacket my father had given me in one of our better moments, and some clothes, and I wore them all when I slept in the broom closet. It was just as hard and cold there as it was outside, and it was winter in Chicago and I was thirteen. I could see my breath pooling in the dark and woke shivering every night. I had a watch, so I knew it was usually three, and then I'd wait until six, when I went to the Laundromat on California

Avenue and would sit there trying to get warm. But after a while I couldn't get warm and even in school I was shivering all the time, vibrating in my big jacket.

But this isn't about school (I was in eighth grade). And it's not about my father handcuffing me to a pipe and leaving me there in the basement of his old house. And it's not about the hotel room I ended up in one homeless evening, with a man in a nurse's uniform and a wig giving head to three larger, stronger men, lines of coke spread haphazardly across the table. All of that is true, but this is just a list of the different places I slept.

I slept at home. I went home several times. I had a large bedroom, and the walls were covered in wallpaper that looked like an open sky full of birds. I had a down comforter and two pillows in Charlie Brown pillowcases. I had a manual typewriter I banged on, and I taped bad poetry over my walls and listened to Pink Floyd albums on the cabinet record player. I made dinner from endless cans of Chef Boyardee and stacks of frozen steaks. If I were to guess, I would say that rapprochements with my father led to me sleeping at home a full month out of the eleven I spent as a homeless child in Chicago. Other friends who ran away would climb in through my window and sleep beneath my bed.

I turned fourteen in a basement I had broken into with my friends Albert and Justin. Justin was often homeless that year too, and he also slept in many places. The floor was blue cement, and we sat up most of the night against the wood storage sheds, working our way through pints of vodka and confessing to things like masturbation. In the morning the police woke us with flashlights and boots and sent us back to the streets.

I slept in the police station, the Twenty-Fourth District, the flat, dark building with the giant parking lot on Clark Street. I was arrested for curfew, then drug possession, then breaking into parking meters. I slept on the scratched steel cot inside the cell in the juvenile unit or sitting upright with my wrist next to my ear, handcuffed to a steel loop in the wall.

A Jewish man found me in the broom closet. He seemed confused. He couldn't understand why a child was sleeping there. He probably owned the building. He was probably just coming to get a mop. "It's OK," I told him, gathering my things in my arms, careful not to look in his eyes, and walking away. I was fourteen. I didn't want to answer obvious questions. The broom closet was locked after that.

On the coldest nights, when my lashes became icicles, I snuck into a boiler room and slept next to the warm pipes and left when I heard the banging that meant someone was coming down the stairs. I walked along Devon Avenue when the bank clock read twenty below. I had hypothermia. It was like a circuit at times: roof, roof, boiler room. Other times things settled and I would go to the same place over and over again and go to sleep just like anyone else.

I slept at my father's girlfriend's apartment, on a couch in her living room, and I watched her sleep through the half-open door to her bedroom, her blanket riding up her naked thighs. She slept flat on her stomach with her head turned, breathing softly into the pillow, and her legs slightly spread. I watched the balls of her feet, the curve of her toes, and her tan calves. This is not about her struggling to hold on to me, arms wrapped around my waist while I lunged for the doorknob, my father on his way, upset over the social workers who had begun to bother him about his homeless child. Or the violence that occurred after he found me walking late that night down Chicago Avenue, covered in snow, and took me home and smacked me across the face and shaved my head.

I slept in my grandparents' small flat outside Sheffield, England. My grandparents are dead now, both of them. They weren't expecting me. I drank barley wine at night with them, and my grandfather told me stories about the Great War and made jokes about his missing thumb. When they went to sleep, I journeyed out to the pubs and I drank some more. During the day I hiked the Uden valley, watched the sheep in the long green fields. I found my first strip club in the back of a small pub with a broken window. Several times I hitchhiked into Sheffield to watch punk-rock bands and met people who were looking for fights. I wasn't looking for a fight. After a week my grandparents sent me back to America.

I slept above the Quick Stop on Pratt and California, only a block away from my grammar school. I climbed the gutters to the roof and lay in the corner beneath the lip to block the wind. Sometimes I would poke my head up and see the lights at the crosswalk and the black, empty streets, and I would feel so lucky and free. There were video games in the store, but I wasn't allowed inside. The teachers knew I was homeless and bought me lunch, but no one offered to take me home. My friends' parents also didn't offer to take me in. At PTA meetings parents were warned to keep their children away from me. I was a known drug user, an eighth-grade drinker, when I could get the money together. One time Justin's father chased me down the sidewalk in his taxi, trying to run me over. When I jumped the fence to get away, he pressed a gun against my friend Roger's chest and commanded him to tell where I was. But Roger didn't know, and that, like so many other things that happened that year, is not what this is about.

I stole food from the dumpster behind the Dominick's, cold packets of meat just past the sell-by date. I slept at the canal, where we built fires and planned adventures, all the neighborhood's forgotten children, the ones whose parents didn't notice they were missing or didn't care, dancing near the flames. Nobody looked for us. We named things. The tree I sat in was called Steve's Office, the fire pit was Pete Brown's Grave. Pat had a throne dug into the dirt below the path, and Rob had Rob's Chair, which was just the tip of a boulder protruding horizontally from the slope. We respected each other's space most of the time. We built a fire every night, and we threw rocks at the rats as they scurried in and out of the filthy water. We had wonderful times at the canal playing heavy-metal music and dropping acid while trying to stay awake for cops and tougher kids who might want to beat us up. One time Fat Mike came running, out of breath. He had seen headlights near the baseball stadium. "Dude," he said. "Could be a cop car, could be a party car, I don't know." We laughed for hours over that. We woke up covered in dirt, reeking of smoke, and went to school.

I slept at home. My mother was dead. My father didn't always notice me when I came back; other times he woke me with a loud whistle. He never reported me missing when I left again. We didn't want each other, and eventually he moved himself to the suburbs with his new wife and didn't bother to get me his forwarding address.

I slept three nights with a Christian man who did painting work for my father. He lived in a small apartment, and his wife was dying rapidly, as my mother had. I went with him to church. I ruined his baking pan cooking hamburger on his stovetop. It wasn't working out, he told me. Years later my father contacted me demanding I write his Christian friend a thank-you letter.

There was a man named Ron. He had an apartment beneath Pat's mother's apartment. Pat's mother was a junkie and Ron was just a twenty-year-old slacker who would one day go to community college and get a degree in hospitality that would allow him to work in a hotel. I had stolen some money and bought a quarter pound of marijuana, and Ron let me stay with him until the marijuana was gone. Pat's mother is dead now. Justin's parents are also dead. Roger's dad is dead. Dan's mom is dead. It has nothing to do with the story, but my friends' parents all died young.

I slept beneath Brian's bed, and when Brian's father caught me, he kicked me out, and then he beat Brian. Brian's father saw me stumbling down the street drunk, with my shirt off in the middle of winter, and he said to his daughter, "I ought to put him out of his misery." He did too much coke and had a bad heart. He died too.

I slept in the closet of an independent-living home for wards of the state. The home was on Sacramento. A normal, boxy-looking house in the middle of the street, with a small basketball court in the backyard. Eight boys lived there, transitioning between group homes and living alone. Some of the boys snuck me inside. The closet was small, and I had to sleep sitting up with my legs crossed. I was discovered by the staff, and they fed me a bowl of cereal. Someday soon the state would take custody of me and I would also be a ward of the state and I would live in that very home for a time.

More often than anything, I slept outside. I slept in parks and in the woods and on the neighborhood rooftops. But when you can fall asleep anywhere, you often do. I was always the last to leave the party. I never had to go home.

Sometimes Justin would have a girlfriend, and I would sleep on the couch and he would sleep in the bedroom. Justin was popular that way. He was beautiful, like a woman, with his long black hair. Sometimes Justin and I slept together on a gravelly rooftop, and he would wrap his thin legs over my legs and his sinewy arms across my chest and hold me tight, his face buried in my neck, and I was never sure if he was doing that because he wanted to or because he thought I expected it from him.

Justin and I slept at the Maxworks, a hippie commune in Jewtown. The neighborhood doesn't exist anymore. They paved it over to expand the university campus. The Maxworks was a three-story abandoned building taken over by radicals, many of whom lived there for twenty years. They smoked dandelions and banana skins and made pocket money selling handmade pipes to the junkies sitting around garbage cans outside. Justin and I were too young to recognize what we had stumbled on: the failure of an earlier generation's promise. They gave us acid—yellow sunshine—and one of the women in a flowery skirt with unshaven legs and armpits had sex with Justin. I don't remember her name, but I remember her spinning in circles in a trash heap near a fire. Her arms were outstretched and her dress was translucent. I was so jealous, but there was nothing I could do about it. I was an ugly child, and sometimes my ugliness kept me safe.

From the Maxworks, over eight days in the summer of 1986, Justin and I slept our way in cars and trucks across America. The truck stop in East Los Angeles was a sea of flashing lights, the air wavy with gasoline, open trailers filled with rolls of carpet, men standing on dock ladders or leaning back in their rigs, chatting lazily on the radio in the deafening hum of the motoring engines. I slept in the cabin of a truck while the driver molested Justin in the front. I slept right through it, and in the morning, sitting in a doughnut shop under a blank gray sky, surrounded by highways and the roar of traffic, Justin told me he wanted to kill that man. He had stolen our only bag, and inside was my poetry and our maps. I thought that was what Justin was talking about, the poetry and the maps, but it wasn't. Years later, when I was at a party telling my favorite story, about hitchhiking from Chicago to California with my best friend, Justin would interrupt me and say, "Steve, I was molested."

"Why didn't you wake me up?" I asked, which was a dumb thing to say. I was so angry.

In Las Vegas we slept in the juvenile detention center. We had caught a ride with a German, and he took us from Los Angeles to the Strip. He wore shorts and drove with a beer between his legs. Good beer, he said, from Germany. He stopped in a convenience store and bought cheap beer so we would have something to drink too. He had a small bong in the glove compartment and a pillbox filled with weed, and we smoked that as we drove into the desert, and he dropped us off at Caesars Palace, where we stocked up on free matchbooks and wondered what to do next.

A state trooper answered that question. We were out on the entry ramp, trying to hitch a ride out of town. Our clothes were muddy and ripped. We were put in jail as runaways. They contacted my father, who stopped in the print shop on Pratt Boulevard and told the woman working there, "They arrested my son in Las Vegas. I'm not going to get him."

"No offense," she told me when I met her years later, "but I didn't give a shit."

I said goodbye to Justin in his small room with white walls on the ground floor of the institution. It was early in the morning, the desert sun rising above the low buildings, and he wasn't quite awake. His dark hair covered his eyes. His gym shoes were in the hallway in front of the red walking line, and he asked why I was being let out first. I told him I didn't know. They drove me to the Greyhound station, and then they took off my handcuffs. I slept on a bus for three days as it snaked slowly across the country from Las Vegas to Chicago. They gave me four dollars when they let me out, and I spent it on cigarettes and candy bars. We stopped at the McDonald's dotting the highway and a state fair in Carbondale. The man next to me fed me whiskey in a coffee cup, and I slept against his shoulder at night. He was fresh out of prison and asked if I would be willing to snatch someone's purse. I said I didn't think I would be very good at that. Justin wouldn't get out for several more weeks, and when he did he would be rearrested on an oustanding warrant and he would go to Audy Home and his parents would refuse to pick him up and the state would take custody of him and he would spend the rest of his childhood in a state home in the Chicago suburbs.

When I got back to Chicago, I slept on the streets, as I had been doing for so long now. I slept on a friend's porch until his mother found out. I slept on the same rooftops. I hooked up with a children's agency, and they put me in Central Youth Shelter. It was a gladiator arena filled with children awaiting placement, stuffed thirty to a room. We sat around during the day watching television or playing basketball in the fenced-in yard. The shelter was understaffed, and nobody would tell me where I was going or when I would get out. Then I walked away.

I slept for a while in a house connected to a Catholic church and in private homes of people who had volunteered to take in children while the state waited the requisite twenty-one days to decide if the state was willing to take custody. There was something wrong with the adults who took me in, all men living alone. I think they were pedophiles and I was a disappointment to them. I played pool with other homeless children at the Advocates Center beneath the Granville train tracks. There was a girl there, a year older than me, tall, thin, and freckled. She always beat me and then did this little victory dance with her hands, fingers stretched like wings. She had the biggest smile.

Then I slept in the house I had grown up in, which my father was in the process of selling. It was an obvious mistake.

I woke into his fists, and I tried to cover my face. He dragged me into the kitchen, where he had clippers, forced me to my knees in front of the cabinet, and shaved my head. It was the second time he did that. There were giant bald patches from where his hands slipped, and I looked like a mental patient, which was ironic. He must have been waiting for me, or searching the neighborhood. He had planned to do this. Revenge for something. The meanest thing possible, worse even than the beating, worse than handcuffing me to a pipe, was to be humiliated in front of everyone. To be a circus freak. It was an act of raw cruelty well within my father's emotional range. Something he felt was owed him for being negatively portrayed as a parent, for the hatred he saw when he looked in my eyes. But that's not what this is about at all. This isn't about hate or love or what went wrong between my father and me or the kind of resentments that never go away. This isn't about splitting the blame between bad parents and bad children. It's not about culpability. It's about sleeping and the things that are important to that, like shelter and rain.

That night was the last night of my homeless year. It was the end of August, and high school would start in a couple of days. I had cut my wrist open, and there was a bright-red gash that bled throughout the afternoon. It was hot, and a festival was under way in the park. A soft breeze cut around the sleigh hill and a few clouds pocked the long sky. I solicited beer, and people bought me beer because they thought maybe I was crazy or maybe they could get me to leave. I asked one man if I could go home with him, and he said, "Look, I bought you a beer," which was true enough. As night fell, a band ascended the stage, and I danced while they played, slamming in the mosh pit at the top of the baseball diamond, my wrist still open, splashing traces of blood on people's clothes. Proof I was there.

I crawled in the entryway of an apartment building across from the park. I didn't care anymore. I slept in the open and I heard footsteps pass and a door closing, and then opening again. The floor was small tiles held together with cement, and the door was a glass case barreled in dark wood. I rested with my head on my arm and my knees pulled toward my chest. I had a sack of clothes somewhere. A friend's parent had given it to me, long white shirts and discarded pants, but I couldn't remember where I'd left them. My jeans were torn, and I wore a black rock-and-roll T-shirt. I knew it was only a matter of time until the door closing became a phone call and the phone call became swirling red and blue lights and the lights became a backseat and a window with bars.

The police came, and they asked where my parents were. I told them I didn't know, which was true. The police weren't mean or angry. They were just doing their job. In the morning I met a different set of officers, who didn't wear uniforms or carry guns. The new officers offered me sandwiches and something to drink. They asked what happened to my wrist, and I told them I fell on a tin can, but they didn't believe me. I was taken to a hospital, and a kind nurse used surgical tape to close the hole in my wrist.

"Why would you do that?" she asked, and I wanted to laugh at her. I wanted to ask if she was offering me a place to stay. But she was just concerned and nice, and I would meet a lot more people like her. Things got much better after that, though it took me a little while to recognize it. Things were going to work out fine, save some scars.

—*Peterborough, New Hampshire, 2005*

My Little Brother Ruined My Life

"Are you a masochist?" It's the first thing Bosco asks me. He's four-teen years old now, almost my height, five eight, creamy white skin, and a small German nose from my stepmother's side of the family. He's wearing pajama bottoms and my father's green bomber jacket. We're in a cab, returning from the airport. He's here to stay with me for ten days. And I'm realizing I've made a terrible mistake.

"Why would you think that?" I ask. I just flew into San Fran-cisco two hours earlier myself. I haven't been home in weeks.

"Dad says you're a masochist. He read it somewhere."

"I'm a fiction writer," I say. "It's fiction."

"Sure it is," he says.

We go to a party for people from the university. Bosco grabs two beers from the fridge and hands me one. "He's a little young to be drinking, isn't he?" Claire asks. Claire's a poet from Georgia. The house is filled with poets and short-story writers. Jackets are piled on the bed in the bedroom, and people are lying on them or on the floor, telling stories about losing their virginity. Everybody has an MFA, so every story has a small, inappropriate observation. "He put his hand between my legs at the movie theater. I was wearing my mother's skirt . . ." "I was fifteen and she was nineteen. It was the day after my best friend committed suicide." My brother hangs on the front steps with Kaui's boyfriend, Andy, and Andy tells him not to do heroin. "Everything else is OK," Andy says.

"That guy was cool," Bosco says.

. . .

I don't know my little brother as well as I should. We've met only a handful of times. I left home before I was his age. My father and I never really mended our relationship. He remarried, made money, moved to the suburbs, had my little brother and sister with his new wife. I wrote a book about growing up in group homes and the violence there. My father thinks I have exaggerated my victimhood at his expense. We get along for months at a time, and then I'll get some note explaining how he wasn't that bad a father, how he didn't shave my head, he gave me haircuts, and I'll remember waking to my father's fists and being dragged along the floor, into the kitchen. My father likes to joke that he only handcuffed me to a pipe that one time, and look how many stories I've gotten out of it. He thinks he should have been a worse father because it would have helped my writing. Sometimes I tell my father it's best we don't talk for a while. So I was surprised when he suggested Bosco come out and stay with me. I was more surprised when, after saying yes, I found out the ticket was ten days away.

What I have to keep telling myself is that Bosco is a kid, and being a kid is hard. I'm not jealous that he's growing up with two parents in a big house in the suburbs. I want to be a good brother, but the truth is that I don't have the skills. I've borrowed a sleeping bag for him; my studio is so small. He sleeps on the wooden floor, his feet inches from my head. His feet smell, and I'm going to have to tell him about that.

"Stop walking into me," I say. We're on Sixteenth Street, and Bosco keeps brushing against me and I keep moving further away until I am against the buildings.

"I'm not. You're walking into me."

"From now on I'm going to call you Underfoot," I say. "You see these lines on the sidewalk? Stay on your side of the line."

"You stay on your side of the line." The streets are crowded and the fruit vendors are out, so it's hard for either of us to stick to our grids. We pass the Victoria Theatre, where *Hedwig and the Angry Inch* is in its final week.

"It's like my feet are magnets and you have a metal head."

We try, we try. We watch a basketball game at my friend's house, and I lose fifty dollars. "What were you thinking?" Bosco asks. "Syracuse is sooo much better."

"You're fourteen years old. You don't know anything about college basketball."

"Neither do you, apparently."

We head to the Orbit Room, where my ex-girlfriend is getting drunk with her friends. I worry that my brother will think I drink too much. Then I worry that maybe I drink too much.

Theresa is wearing blue jeans and a torn black shirt. It's always tough to see an ex-girlfriend and realize she's getting better-looking. Theresa has been at the protests all day in Oakland. "They fired rubber bullets at us," she says proudly. "It was amazing."

The Orbit Room has round cement tables that are four feet high, and people sit around them on tall stools. Bosco is off talking to someone. I say to Theresa, "This is awful. It's like coming face to face with a part of yourself you had no interest in knowing."

"You'll do fine," she says.

"No," I tell her. "I don't like children. Also, my apartment is too small. And I've been sick recently, I have this ringing in my ears."

"Don't think about yourself," Theresa says. "Think about your brother."

"Why do I have to think about him?" I ask. "He has everything. Can we stay with you?"

"No. I'm getting on with my life."

It's almost one in the morning and we're walking home. "Why'd you break up with her?" Bosco asks. "She's the whole package." He sounds like my father. My father always spoke of women as if they were frozen meat.

"Yeah, she's great," I say, and I think of how if I hadn't broken up with her, we would be at her place now. Bosco would be in her extra bedroom, and I would be on the inside of the spoon.

"You'll never get a girlfriend like that again."

A child sleeps on my floor. The morning is full of rain. I watch my hands as I type. I have scars up and down my wrist from all my suicide attempts.

My father writes to say that my fourteen-year-old cousin went to one concert and became a doper, and now my uncle is going to throw him out. This is why I hate email. I tell my father that I was doing dope long before my first concert and that maybe my uncle should be a little more thoughtful in assigning blame. My father tells me my uncle has a family to think about. This is my father's favorite notion. The idea that a family must abandon one of its own for the good of the whole. That's why he moved while I was living on the streets, he says. Because I was a drug addict and he had to think of the family. Which is why, when the police found me after a year on the streets, and asked where my parents were, I answered that I didn't know. Honestly, I didn't. But my family was just two people then, my father and my sister. So I've always been skeptical of that argument. I've always been skeptical of parents who abandon children for the good of the family.

I introduce Bosco to Amber, a sixteen-year-old girl from the writing program where I volunteer as a tutor. We go to a movie that isn't very good and then dessert at an overpriced coffee shop. "So how long are you here for?" Amber asks Bosco.

"Until next Sunday."

"Wow. A whole week more." Amber is young and pretty. She's an A student, the editor of her school newspaper. She can make Bosco into a better person. Young boys are so easy to manipulate. They think of only one thing. Someday, when he's older, Bosco will also think of his place in the world and how people don't appreciate him enough. He'll worry about how hard it is to make a living. He'll feel jealousy and anger when he is passed over for a promotion and then self-loathing for his own small-mindedness.

Amber takes Bosco back to her home in the Haight. I take the opportunity to get some work done, push his things into the back of the studio, and do the dishes. When he comes home we both have one of those Smirnoff Ice drinks that I have in my fridge.

"What did you guys talk about?" I ask.

"Drugs, mostly."

"Yeah?"

"Yeah. She likes to do mushrooms."

"Oh. Yeah, mushrooms are good. When I was your age I loved acid."

"My friend does acid," he says.

"Acid is bad for you," I tell him. Though I know I'm too late. I can tell he's going to become a horrible drug addict and imagine the next time he visits he'll steal my laptop and sell it for crack.

"She said I was weird." He's leaning against the wall, below the lip of the window. I live on a busy street. Dirt from exhaust pipes builds up along the base. My little brother has something more to say. He has that kid smile. He thinks he's so cool. I raise my eyebrow.

"I shook her hand, but she wanted a hug," he says. "I might have been able to score, but I didn't try."

My brother and I have card-playing ancestry. Our grandfather played cards every day of his adult life. He was an absentee father. He worked during the day and played cards at night. My uncle said he nearly gambled away their house. Because I'm the best euchre player at the university, people are always trying to take me down a peg. I get paired up with my brother.

"That's a spade," I say, pointing to the jack of clubs.

"No, it isn't." He's on his third beer. He's sucking them down like water. Perhaps he'll be an alcoholic before he turns eighteen. Everybody's half-drunk, and they holler at Bosco to bring them drinks. He's become the beer boy.

"It is a fucking spade."

"Why are you swearing at your brother?"

"When spades are trump, the jack of the same color becomes the second highest trump."

"You should have told me," he says. He turns everything back that way.

"I did tell you."

"No, you didn't."

"Why don't you just admit you're wrong?" I say. "Why don't you take responsibility for your actions?"

"Why don't you admit you're wrong?"

"Your grandfather would turn over in his grave if he saw you playing cards that way."

After one more beer apiece, Bosco and I stumble home, arm in arm. The restaurants are closed; the world is asleep. "That's nothing," Bosco says, peeing on the wall of a live-work loft building. "Me and my friend Jimmy drank a whole bottle of whiskey. I don't get hungover."

"That's one more thing you can look forward to."

He'll be leaving in a few days, and we haven't done anything. We haven't seen either bridge, Golden Gate Park, the ocean, or the bay. We haven't been to any museums. We haven't hiked Lands End or gone rock climbing. When people ask him what he did in San Francisco, Bosco will say he got drunk. But the thing is, I don't have a television. I don't have PlayStation. I don't have Internet. There is absolutely nothing to do in my apartment except read, write, and get drunk. There's a message on the machine from my father. "I just wanted to check in on my boys, make sure you're having a good time." Anyway, there are only a few days left, and

I'm counting them off. Walking near Polk Street, I offer to pay for Bosco to go to bed with a transvestite prostitute.

"Shut up," he says.

"You won't notice the difference," I tell him.

"You're sick."

"I'm going to tell everybody you did it anyway, and they'll believe me because I'm older than you."

It's late on Thursday night, and there's been a party at the tutoring center, with raffles and piñatas. Friends of mine are drinking at the bar, but they won't let Bosco in. Bosco says I should go without him; he'll wander the Mission District. I tell him I don't think that's a good idea. We stop to see Theresa at a reading in a used-book store.

"I'm leaving him with you. I'm going out."

"Like hell you are." She's wearing a charcoal-gray skirt. Her legs are tight and tanned, swimmer's legs. I slip my foot under her foot, which dangles off the armrest of a comfy chair. She moves it away. There's a blond boy with her, smiling awkwardly.

"Let's all go back to your place," I say. "I'll buy."

"You'll buy what?"

"Anything. I don't care."

"No. I'm doing things."

"What kind of things?"

"This is Sherman."

"Hello, Sherman."

Later, at the Pakistani restaurant near Guerrero, we split rice, naan, and an order of chicken tikka masala. "I take back what I said about her," Bosco says. "She's not that nice." He's on my side.

Bosco wants to go to a concert with Amber and her friends, but I say no, not unless I chaperone. Bosco says please, so I tell him we'll have to ask his parents. We call, and they say no. He calls my stepmother back and begs her. "Why?" he says. "That's stupid. But, Mom. But, Mom." He hangs up the phone.

"Did you just hang up on your mother?"

"Yes."

We meet the girls at the station, and I find myself wanting to impress them, but I can't. Young girls talk a lot, act dramatic, dance around and sing inside trains. I feel so old.

The club is near the warehouses and the waterfront. Teenagers are sprawled across the sidewalk. I go inside, sway to the punk music. I want to dance, but I don't want to be the old dancing guy.

The first band poured motor oil on the floor so people could slide while they listened to the music. I help the clean-up crew mop the mess, and Bosco disappears with some of the girls. When he comes back, he's smiling, and I think he's stoned.

"Don't worry," Amber says. "We'll take care of him. You can leave him with us."

I say no, I'll stick around. I go to the bar across the street for a drink.

On the way to the train, Bosco walks with his new friend Mickey. It makes me happy to see him bonding. These are good kids, except that they are stoners and two years older than him. They are very kind children, environmentalists. They don't think guns are cool. And that's what I want for Bosco, to introduce him to kids who don't think violence is a good thing. Because his uncle has closets full of guns and swastika tattoos, and his cousin was given a shotgun for his fourteenth birthday. It's after midnight now, and parents are calling these children, who are out so late, on their cell phones. The children say they are doing fine.

I think of my own mother, who died painfully for five years on the living room couch. She used to pee in a bucket, and I would have to walk her pee to the bathroom and flush it in the toilet. "Give me money," I would tell her. And she would refuse, so I would yell and scream. And then she would give in, because she was too ill and weak to fight. Then my father stopped giving her money. Sometimes I would yell at her, and other times I would curl up with her, laying my head on the quilted blanket covering her legs. I remember loving her and hating her. I remember how often she cried. Despite what people might say, I don't think she liked me very much in the end. Children are horrible. Children are monsters.

And yet most people my age have them. I do too, I think. I was a sperm donor for about a year when I was living in my car. I checked the box that said they can look me up when they turn eighteen. Fifteen years from now, I expect to meet the genetic experiment I made at forty-five dollars a toss in the Berkeley clinic.

It's one in the morning. Bosco says he wants to stay out with Mickey and Amber, and I say OK. I give him forty dollars and tell him to take a cab home.

Back in the apartment I watch the dangerous city from my window. I can see a chocolate factory and Twin Peaks and the lights of the cars driving up the hills. Bosco calls. He's having a good time. His friends are having dinner in a twenty-four-hour diner. I used to wait tables in a place like that. I know the kind of kids that come in at two in the morning. They have too much freedom. "We're going to Liz's place in West Portal," Bosco tells me.

"No," I tell him.

"C'mon."

"Use the money I gave you to get in a cab. It's time to come home."

On Bosco's last night we go to Andrew's to play cards. First we watch *Orgazmo* at Ben's house. Then we walk Valencia to Dolores

Park and I point across my adopted city to the San Francisco–Oakland Bay Bridge. "You see," I say, "it's so much more colorful here than in Chicago."

"And that's a good thing?"

"There are more parks. Did you know there's more park per square foot than in any other major city?"

"I'm hungry. When are we going to eat?"

"Did you have fun while you were here?"

"It beats being in school."

At Andrew's, there are so many people that we have to split into two games of cards. I tell Bosco I'm going to set a good example for him by not drinking tonight, but I have a few beers anyway. Bosco wants to know if he can drink too, and I tell him he can have a beer if more than half the people in attendance say it's OK. "This is democracy," I say. He's too shy to ask.

Bosco partners with Adam, and I partner with Geoff. He wins every game, and I win every game, and in the end it's Geoff and I against Adam, my brother, and Tom. The score's nine to six. Geoff and I are in the barn. "Should I call it?" Bosco asks Adam, and Adam spreads his large hands and says, "Last time you called that you got euchred."

"I think we should," Bosco says. He's got that look in his eye, the look of a gambler. We're not playing for money, but somewhere inside his head the little synapses are firing. He has a keen understanding of the game for his age, a rational mind, an ability to learn from his mistakes, but he does not have the ability to read other people, and he doesn't take instruction well. I slow-play a king of trump, and when Geoff takes it with the left bower, I lay down the rest of my cards. Game over.

"That's a great game," Bosco says on the way home. "I only lost to you tonight."

"You'll never beat me in cards," I tell him. "It's your burden to bear."

· · ·

I wanted to steer my brother in the right direction. Instead we drank and played cards. Sunday morning the streets are still wet.

"Is there anything I can do to convince you to stay?" I ask.

"You'd have to give me more money."

"You've already spent all my money."

"Oh," he says. "Thanks."

When the big red van pulls up, we put his bag in the back. I go to hug and he goes to slap hands, and we end up in this awkward embrace, with our biceps against each other's necks. "You choked me," he says, climbing into his seat. I point my index finger at him with my thumb up, as if that were some kind of cool sign. The driver gives me a small nod and closes the door. My little brother looks into his lap, fiddling with his CD Walkman. I step back toward the metal grating of my entryway. The driver smiles at me like everything is going to be OK. Like he knows this is my little brother and he understands my concern and will take good care of him and get him to the airport safely, and once at the airport, the boy will board a plane that will not crash, and he will get home fine. And then Bosco will tell the whole world how cool his big brother is, and his father will leave me messages saying how much better I am at this child-raising thing than he was. And I won't return his messages, because my father and I still have so many unresolved issues, but I'll know and he'll know I'm right and I've been right all along. I see all of this in the driver's calming, placid eyes. But he doesn't know anything, he's just a van driver.

—San Francisco, 2003

Hate to Be Alone

On the fourth day we broke up. We had planned this for a while. Not the breakup but the four days. Her husband wanted to spend a week with her over Christmas in Chicago, and so she wanted to spend four days with me when they returned to the Bay Area. That was the deal they worked out.

We had been dating for more than five months, and her marriage was falling apart. Lissette was in an open marriage, where you can see other people, the kind everybody says doesn't work. Except her husband didn't see other people. Which was fine, because they had different desires, but then I came along and we fell in love, and in the nine years she'd been with her husband, she had never fallen in love with someone else. Her husband told her he felt ripped off. She told me he hated me, but I didn't think it was my responsibility. It was the situation that was killing him. I was incidental. Anyway, I had my own problems.

We spent almost the entire four days in bed, and when we broke up there were condoms on the floor, latex gloves covered in lube, a rattan cane flecked with blood. There was rope spread under the desk and near the closet and attached to the bed frame. There was a roller box full of clamps and clothespins and collars and wrist cuffs, and a gas mask and leather hood pulled from under the bed, so we had to step over it when we got up to go to the bathroom. There was a strap-on dildo and holster sitting on top of a box of photographs next to the door, a purple silicone butt plug near the radiator.

·   ·   ·

Love is a hard thing to explain. I had successfully not fallen in love so many times that when Lissette told me she was married, I didn't even flinch. We were in a café, and she was wearing all black. It was the first time we met. She mentioned her husband, said he was away for a couple of days. "I tell him everything," she said. "I told him we were meeting for coffee." She wanted to be sure I understood that he was her primary, that I could never be first in her life.

Two and a half weeks later, I was sitting on her kitchen floor while she prepared dinner—slicing eggplants, soaking them in salt, and transferring them to the stove. The flames licked the bottom of the pot, and I was careful not to move. I didn't want to get in the way. She leaned down and took my face in her hands.

"Look at me," she said. "I love you."

"I love you too," I replied.

The breakup didn't come out of nowhere. I had lost my mind in the week she was in Chicago. I called friends I hadn't seen in years just so I could tell them my story: that I was in love with a married woman and I slept with her once a week and the other six nights I slept alone. My thoughts were consumed with her, and I couldn't do my work. My savings were nearly depleted. I lost my adjunct position at the university when I failed to show up for two classes. I saw her two other days each week in the morning, while her husband was at work, and on days we spent apart, we spoke for an hour on the phone. Sometimes I saw her on the weekend as well and we went dancing and she came back to my house to sleep over, a bonus night. I told my friends I saw her more than her husband did, as if that counted for something.

They said, "Get rid of her."

I said, "What if it's me? What if I'm not capable of love?" And what I meant was that I was thirty-four years old, and I had never been in a serious relationship in my entire life. I had never been in love. There was no one in the world who depended on me in any way.

Before we broke up she told me the story of meeting her husband. They had been neighbors. She had a boyfriend and lived with him downstairs, and her would-be husband lived upstairs with his wife. They rarely spoke. She usually spoke with the wife, and he spoke with the boyfriend. But years later he was divorced from his wife, and Lissette was no longer with her boyfriend, and he called and asked, Would she like to go see a band? He'd fathered a child since the last time they had met.

He didn't try anything that first date, because he's a gentleman, with his short, dark hair and innocent face. He's tall and thin, straight-shouldered, and from a good family with a good name. He works in a brokerage, wears a suit to work and a black leather jacket. He asked her on a second date and then asked what her deal was. She explained that she was seeing someone, this guy. But the guy had moved to Seattle. So now they were still together, but she was seeing other people as well. She said she liked seeing other people. She didn't believe in seeing only one person, in constraining love. She was never going to be monogamous again; she had tried, and it made her unhappy. This was Northern California—a woman's body was her own, and people didn't have to abide by the old rules if they didn't want to. He asked if he could be one of those other people she was seeing, and she said yes, and six months later they were living together and then they were married, and she became a mother to his son.

We had almost broken up on the first day, three days before our breakup. I was badly damaged and trying to hide it when I arrived to pick her up at her house. Why was I so sad? I thought it was the holidays. Christmas is my least favorite day of the year. And my girlfriend had been away with her husband. And we'd had a fight before she left. And my friends were also out of town.

Christmas was over; it was cold, and the streets were wet. It was eight in the morning and I was on time but not early, because her husband left for work at seven thirty and he and I had already run into each other too many times. They owned a small ranch house built in the backyard of a larger house. Their bedroom was dominated by a king-size bed with a short space between two large dressers. Her husband's laundry sat in a small pile in the corner, and I waited there while Lissette showered.

She had been miserable in Chicago, where the streets were so cold and her feet hurt from walking the city. She said they'd been to the library and the museum, the Art Institute, and Clark and Division. They'd taken a train to Addison and seen Wrigley Field. I'm from Chicago, and I held my tongue because I thought they had missed everything.

Later that day, in my room—which is just a yellow space I rent in someone else's apartment and is filled with everything I own in the whole world, because I own so little—before the box full of sex toys was all the way out from under the bed and maybe there were just one or two gloves on the floor, she told me she didn't think it could work. And we broke up. But then she changed her mind. In the morning she broke up with me again, and again changed her mind. We never left the bed.

I told a joke about Arabs sending threatening email in order to get the federal government to come out and dig up their yard for them.

On the third day we didn't break up. She caned me, then tied me spread-eagle to the bed and got on top of me. "Don't come," she said. And then we lay in bed talking about how much we loved each other and the various things we had done together. It was a list that included Nashville and honky-tonk bars and packed lunch on cliffs overlooking San Francisco Bay. We'd been to readings and parades and movies and shopped for organic produce at an Asian grocery in Berkeley. We always held hands. We'd been dancing, and we danced together well. We spent hours on the phone agreeing on the political issues of the day. Beneath it was this: We were sexually compatible. She liked to hurt people, and I liked to be hurt. She liked it when I cried, and I wanted to cry all the time.

She turned me over and tied my arms forward and spread my legs and bound a rope around my ankles and thighs to keep my knees bent and greased her strap-on and slid it inside me. "I'm not going to go easy," she said. "I want to hear you."

When we were done, she said, "I did all the things you like today."

"You did," I told her. She asked me why I thought she did these things, and I said because she loved me, and I told her I loved her too.

We went out that night. The only time in four days we left the bed. But not for long. We went to a noodle house with small round tables, and I looked at other couples on dates or just eating dinner. Everyone was in pairs; no one was eating alone. There were couples who had just met, trying to impress each other, still hiding themselves, afraid of what the other might think if the other saw them whole. Older couples were there, people who had been together many years and had stopped talking altogether. Each person in each couple had their own unique needs. I wondered what those needs were and if they were being met. A famous analyst was once asked, "What would you call an interpersonal relationship where infantile wishes, and defenses against those wishes, get expressed in such a way that the persons within that relationship don't see each other for what they objectively are but, rather, view each other in terms of their infantile needs and their infantile conflicts?"

"I'd call that life," he replied.

From the noodle house we went to a bar. There were people I knew at the bar, and they were playing darts. One of them was moving to France to finish a novel he'd been working on for years. I didn't want to know about it. I thought the bar was cold and empty and there was too much space.

On the fourth day we broke up for real.

It was 1:40 in the afternoon, and the curtains were open. We could see my neighbor sitting at a computer in a square of light on the fourth floor of the apartment building across the street. Lissette asked if I remembered when we first got together, and she told me how she was territorial and jealous, and I had said I could be monogamous with her. She told me she was consumed with jealousy. It wasn't a matter of me seeing other women; she was burning with the idea that I might desire them, which I didn't deny. She had never felt this kind of jealousy before.

I told her I didn't know what I wanted, because I had never been in a relationship like this. I didn't know what it would do to me. I didn't say what I thought, which was that this was about other things. That we both wanted our lives back. I wanted to write and she wanted to save her marriage and I wanted to find someone who would love me all the time, even though I doubted I would. Even though I knew that sharing her part-time was more than I would ever get full-time with someone else. We had stopped growing. Everything had stopped.

Our four days were two hours and twenty minutes from ending. She was meeting her husband in Union Square. They were going to go shopping and then maybe see a movie. It was New Year's Eve tomorrow, and she wanted to get groceries so she could have a traditional New Year's Day breakfast, with fish and rice, to start the new year correctly with friends. Earlier in our relationship she mentioned that she hoped we could get to where I could come over for New Year's and be comfortable with her husband and he with me. But we never got to that point. I never fully joined her harem with her husband, who had stayed true to his wife these nine years while she went through a parade of men, looking to see if it was possible to love two men at the same time and finally deciding on me. Maybe it was the sex. She rarely had sex with her husband. He wasn't into the kinky things we were into. He hadn't grown up eroticizing his childhood trauma the way I had. And he had married a sadist.

She said she couldn't do it, and I agreed. Then I waited a heart-beat, and I said, "So we're breaking up?" And this time I knew it was true because I started to cry and she grabbed me and I buried my face inside her hair.

"I can't leave you," she said.

"I don't want to be without you," I said.

"Then don't be."

But five minutes later I asked what was going to happen, and she said we were done, and I nodded. Still, we stayed in bed.

"Don't cry," she said. I'd cried in front of her so many times over five months. At first I had been embarrassed, but then I realized she liked it, so I cried freely. I was shocked by my own propensity for tears. I didn't know I had so many of them and they were so close to the surface. I would cry when she was hitting me and she wouldn't stop. She would beat me until the tears were gone and I relaxed again and I came back to her. She said she wanted to provide a space for that little boy inside me. But now she didn't want me to cry anymore, and I tried to put the tears back into wherever they came from.

I knew I was making my own decision. There were things I could say to keep it going, and I wasn't saying them.

I reached into that tub next to the bed and grabbed a condom from a paper bag. I fucked her hard and fast and in a way unlike how I had ever fucked her before. She began to scream, and then her own tears came, drenching her face until she resembled ·

a mermaid. This was our due. We were breaking up and we were entitled to this sex and we were going to have it. It was like fucking in a storm. I gripped the flesh of her thighs. I sniffed at her neck. "C'mon," I said, and she screamed and shook. Then we rolled over and she was on top of me, with her fingers in my hair and one hand on my throat. We were still fucking. She pinched my nipple hard, she reached down between my legs. It didn't matter. I wasn't going to come.

"I want to come," I said.

"OK," she whispered.

"I can't come inside you."

She got off me. We were running out of time. I lay next to her and masturbated quickly and came into the rubber. She pulled the rubber off of me, tying a knot in one swift motion, pulling the end with her thumb and forefinger, striding across the room while I watched the naked triangle of her legs tapering into her ankles.

She tried to call her husband. She didn't want to meet him downtown, she wanted to meet him at home. But he had already left the bank.

"I have to shower," she said.

"He's your husband," I told her. "You don't need to shower for him. He's seen you dirty before."

"I'm not showering for him," she said.

I followed her into the bathroom. My shower was small, with barely enough room for the two of us. We used the scented soap she bought me. This one was composed of dark-brown and white blocks and thin lines, and the bar separated into its parts while we were scrubbing.

"I have to go," she said.

"I can't walk you to the train," I told her. "I don't want to break down at the station."

I got dressed while she dressed. I pulled on my jeans and an undershirt and a T-shirt. I laced up my gym shoes.

"Why are you getting dressed if you're not walking me to the train station?" she asked.

"I don't know," I said.

It was raining, and I offered her my umbrella. The umbrella cost six dollars. I considered giving her my necklace, but I knew she wouldn't wear it. She turned down the umbrella. She was going to get wet. We moved toward the door of my room. She was wearing her long wool coat.

"Don't go," I said suddenly. I didn't even know where it came from, and my hand was in the pocket of her coat and her hand was along my neck and the back of my head. I could have turned into an animal, a dinosaur. I could have grown a giant tail and swung it and broken the windows and the table legs and smashed the bed to pieces.

"Walk me out," she said.

I walked her downstairs, out the front to the entryway of the building. I lit her cigarette on the steps. We kept having one more kiss. She was going to be very late to meet her husband.

—*San Francisco, 2006*

Sometimes I Think About Suicide

In early April, just as the snow is finally melting and the sun's making an appearance in the gray sky, I feel a thought buzzing around in my head. I know what I'm about to do, and I marvel in disbelief at my own powerlessness. Then I smile and walk calmly toward the shadow.

It's not desire. It's like a twitch that moves around my face: Once I've stopped wrinkling my nose, I realize I'm biting the inside of my cheek. After I get that under control, I can't stop blinking and furrowing my eyebrows.

If it's the evening, I say I'll quit in the morning. And in the morning I think, Since I'm not going to do it anymore, maybe I'll do it one last time. Then I try to write, but the work isn't going well. I wonder if I am still a writer, and if I'm not a writer, what am I?

Anyway, the rent is paid, and nothing's due for a while. Then I do that thing again that I'd supposedly just done for the last time. The day leaks away like air from a slowly deflating tire. Sitting at the window, I notice the sky has changed from gray to the color of a bruise. The phone rings, but I don't answer it; they can always call back later. If you're missing often enough, people don't think of you as missing anymore.

When my eyes drift to the digital clock at the corner of the computer screen, it's two a.m. I've barely moved all day. Maybe tomorrow will be better. But tomorrow I'm back at it.

．　．　．

In Ukraine two tall, older girls force an awkward, smaller girl to drink from a puddle. In Taipei, on a dirt plot between giant buildings lit as if on fire, a group of men and women make a scared girl take off all her clothes. In Vietnam a girl delivers a devastating kick to another girl's face. In China five women beat and strip another woman in the middle of a busy street.

I first came across the videos while trying to find a sound effect for an autobiographical film I was writing and directing. The movie is about sexual abuse in state-run group homes like the ones I used to live in. I don't remember the first video I found, but it led to another, and then another. Days passed. Then weeks.

There are two types of videos I watch: fighting and humiliation. The fight videos are mostly on YouTube, but YouTube deletes the most extreme, as well as any that show nudity. The most vicious beatings are reposted on the dark web, which can't be searched with a conventional browser, but they're as easy to find as a twenty-four-hour bodega in Manhattan. Those are the sites that host videos of beheadings, car crashes, suicides, murders, rapes.

I've had four major depressions in my life, the first when I was thirteen, then when I was twenty-four, then again when I was thirty-eight, and now this one, at forty-two. It's scary to think they might be coming closer together, like contractions.

In one video, a woman in Poland catches a friend sleeping with her husband. She slaps the mistress's cheek and forces her to remove her clothes. The mistress begs for mercy. Some unseen person laughs behind the camera. The wife begins cutting the mistress's hair. When it's too short to cut anymore, the wife shaves the woman's head with electric clippers, occasionally swinging her open hand into the mistress's pretty face. Then she kicks the woman in the side of the head and the lower back. The mistress is dragged naked from the room, and the video cuts to her in the back of a car, wrapped in blankets, head unevenly shaved, eyes swollen and dark. The video was probably taken with a phone, a single shot except for that one cut near the end. The video is low quality and eight minutes long.

If I told my therapist about my fascination with this particular video, he might point out that when I was a teen, my father beat me and shaved my head twice, and each time I subsequently tried to kill myself. The second attempt put me in the hospital and left those scars on my left wrist. I barely look at them anymore.

At first I felt something erotic, watching the violence. My mind seemed to go dark as three women attacked a girl's mother and beat her to the ground while the girl watched. Soon it ceased being erotic; it was just dead time, like falling asleep during a staring contest.

I told a friend about the videos. As I was talking, I started to feel nauseous. She tried to remind me I hadn't actually hurt anyone. People watch boxing and the Ultimate Fighting Championship, she said. People watch *The Texas Chain Saw Massacre* and *Saw II*. And it wasn't like I was downloading child porn.

I hate it when someone tries to help me see myself in a better light but I know in my heart they're wrong. I wondered: Was I manipulating her? Was there anything at all she could have said to help me make sense of what was happening?

I tried to explain the different types of videos: maximum damage versus maximum shame.

"Which do you like more?" she asked.

"Humiliation," I said, without needing to think about it.

I'd probably watched at least a thousand videos. Was I upset because of what I was watching, or because of my inability to stop watching it? Did I resent being a moth, or did I resent the flame for drawing me to it?

My friend and I were seated in a courtyard behind a café, and there was a tree arcing toward us, its bark a foamy white mess, the backs of its leaves black as ink. This place has rotted, I thought. Then I went home and searched for more videos. I didn't want to do that, but I did it.

Sometimes when I watched guys fighting in the videos, I could actually feel one of them getting hit. But I was not especially drawn to watching boys fight, even though I could relate.

One spring, when I was twelve or so, I saw one boy get another boy down on the asphalt outside the Quick Stop and kick him for what seemed like twenty minutes.

When I was thirteen, I was beaten by a police officer.

My friend Paul was beaten outside of our school, his arms held at his sides as two kids took swings at his face.

I once smacked a boy named Patrick so hard, he fell on his back.

Like many cowards, I'm drawn to confrontation. I stood up to some threats but backed down from others. I was bullied, but I was also a bully. Once, my roommate in the group home stood over my bed, daring me to move. Jay chased me down California Avenue in the middle of the night until I retreated into a vestibule, and he broke the glass window in the door. Ogie stole my drug money. Tom stole my drugs and kicked me down the stairs.

When I was twenty, I punched an Englishman outside a live sex show in Amsterdam. When I was twenty-two, I grabbed someone by the throat and threw him to the floor in a Florida nightclub, twice. The second time, he got up and punched me in the eye. Afterward I stared at myself in the bathroom mirror, covered in blood.

When I was younger, the violence in my life seemed normal. As I got older, it didn't seem normal anymore because I was hanging out with a different crowd. My new friends hadn't gotten into fights or been beaten and humiliated by a parent. People told me I'd had an awful childhood.

My ex-girlfriend Toni flew in from Colorado to visit me in Brooklyn for two days. Toni and I were supposed to go to a fetish party at a dungeon in Manhattan, but she wasn't feeling well. I had to go into the city anyway for a friend's birthday, so I went without her.

At the birthday party I met a civil-rights attorney who wore faux leather pants and told me about the inner workings of the immigration department. I told her about the fetish party I was going to later. I said I was going to dress up in a negligee with nude stockings and pink heels. The stockings had stars on them.

"Let me see," she said, and I pulled them from my backpack and showed her under the table.

The attorney and a friend of hers followed me upstairs to watch me change into my outfit. "Lift the negligee," she said. "Spin around." She spanked me a few times, not very hard, and then the three of us sat and talked. I felt embarrassed and vulnerable but also really comfortable.

I arrived at the fetish party in my slip and heels, bringing coffee and a sandwich for a dominatrix I know. Like my ex, she was visiting from out of town. We hung out for a while, but she had a client who wanted a strap-on session, so she disappeared into a back room with her coffee and sandwich and dildo harness.

The place was packed. I wandered around and saw my friend Hito, another dominatrix. Her date was a little guy dressed like Robin Hood. She ordered me to stand up straight. Her nails were filed into points, like claws. She pressed one nail underneath my chin as if it were a knife and dug another into my chest until I thought she might break the skin.

"I'm with someone now, and I don't want you to cause any trouble," she said in my ear.

What kind of trouble would I cause? I thought. But of course she was right. I was more than capable of starting trouble.

When I got home, Toni was sitting on the floor near the door, right next to the computer, where I spent most of my time. I wanted to tell her about the videos, but to do that would have implied that I had some control over watching them.

She was wrapped in a blanket and shivering quietly, like a bird, her long black hair spilling over her shoulders. She wasn't going to sleep in the bed with me, she said. She seemed to want to be as far away from me as possible. I wondered what happened to us.

A friend once told me you can never trust someone's account of their own failed relationship. It's like when two objects in space pass each other: you can't tell which one is moving and which one is standing still.

The next night I was supposed to meet Hito at a club on the Lower East Side. I wore a peach-colored slip, with my toenails painted to match, nude pantyhose with colorful squares printed on them, and the pink heels. But it wasn't like the previous night's fetish party. This was a goth party, and everyone was young and wearing black clothes and fishnets and eyeliner, including the boys. There were face tattoos and face piercings. The music was very loud. And of course Hito didn't show. I'd expected as much, which might have been why I was there: hoping to be humiliated and disappointed when she stood me up.

So this is what it's come to, I thought. I'm the old guy at the goth club, alone in a pink dress.

Standing there, watching all the young goths, I thought about writers I knew who'd once seemed to be on a similar career trajectory as mine but were now more successful than I was. Some were writing television shows. One had written a children's book and gotten rich. Another had two kids and a husband and a small but comfortable house in Portland, Oregon. I felt the smooth stockings against my legs and thought: My peers are becoming more normal; I'm just getting weirder.

I was moving further and further away from everyone else. Quite often recently I had thought about suicide—not seriously, but in a way that made me feel as if my time was limited.

A young woman approached me. "You look like a sissy slut," she said.

"Yes," I said, but my voice was so quiet and the music was so loud that I don't think she heard me.

She had an Afro and wore a corset and something like a black swimsuit. Her name was Leila. She pulled me to the bar and made me buy her a drink. Then I knelt and cleaned her boots with my tongue, and she hit me with a belt and tore my stockings and reached between my legs and squeezed hard. Later I laid my head in her lap.

It turned out she was one of the dancers in the show. We exchanged numbers, and I watched her climb onstage to perform. In my six-inch heels, I could see over everybody else. She was a good dancer but she was drunk. I was a good dancer too, but I wasn't really dressed for it in those shoes.

I stood in my torn stockings. I smiled at people occasionally, my slip stuck to my back by some sticky liquid I'd picked up rolling around on the bar floor.

This is my problem, I thought. I belong here.

My job involved writing, but the minute I pulled up to the computer, I'd click on a video instead, and in that way weeks would pass. It was like some science-fiction movie where you go into a chamber and close your eyes and open them a month later.

I'd sold the movie rights to one of my books, and I had enough money to live on for the next two years—maybe a little less. Most of my writer friends taught, which kept them anchored to the world. They also had husbands and wives and kids. Even houses. I might be unfairly characterizing them. Everyone's life is filled with strange hidden cabinets and unopened closets. Still, I was forty-two years old. (I'm forty-four as I finally finish this.) My friends, for the most part, were grown-ups.

Sometimes I would start writing in the morning, and it would go OK for a couple of hours. I'd take a pill for my mood and another to help me concentrate. Then the pills would wear off. I didn't know what I wanted to write, so even if I got something down on the page, it didn't amount to much.

Often in the middle of the day, or occasionally closer to six, I'd start crying. I'd lie in bed and feel the water pooling in my eyes and then sliding down the sides of my face. The last time this had happened was about four years earlier: I'd cried every day for two months. I'd sought help then, and one of the doctors evaluating me had suggested I check myself into the hospital. "I can't go to the hospital," I said. "I have to go to Detroit." I had just gotten a magazine assignment, and I needed the money.

That crying spell had eventually passed, but this time it felt different. I didn't think I was going to come out of it. And anyway, come out of it into what?

At first I thought the most violent videos were all from Eastern Europe and South America, but really people are terrible all over. Like in Philadelphia, where a woman knocks a pregnant woman unconscious, screaming, "You're going to die today, bitch!" and continues to kick her in the head until she's pulled away. Or where one girl takes another into the bathroom at knifepoint and pees on her.

A gang invades a girl's house while her parents are away. A drunk woman crawls along the floor, but no one will let her leave.

A scared high-school girl, naked and surrounded in the locker-room shower, proceeds to hit herself in the face while everyone laughs. It's like she's saying, There's nothing you can do to me that's worse than what I'll do to myself. But even the viewer can see it isn't true. The worst is always yet to come.

It was closing in on Halloween, and the weather was getting colder. I kept thinking about suicide, but I didn't know who to talk to about it. I had a therapist. He was still in training and was therefore affordable, though I never actually paid him—at least, I hadn't in a while. I had some friends, but I didn't see them very often, and it didn't seem appropriate to burden them. What I wanted was a conversation, so I could consider the options, just talk it out:

"So the thing is, yesterday the sadness came on big, the way a breeze becomes a squall, and I cried for two hours and started looking up methods of suicide."

This is the part you're afraid to talk about.

"Yes. This is where it gets real: when the depressed person starts figuring out how they are going to do it. I was on Wikipedia, researching the different ways. You know, in the U.S., the most common way to kill yourself is with a gun, but in Hong Kong people jump from the tops of buildings. Very few people jump from bridges, even though it seems romantic. Almost every way of killing yourself is either very painful or you risk surviving with a serious impairment. And, as you know, I don't have a life that would work very well with a serious impairment. No one would take care of me."

The loneliness is part of your justification.

"Yes, but it's also true."

Go on.

"There is this one method: It's called a suicide bag. It's just a bag with a Velcro strap and a helium container or something.

Basically the gas knocks you out, and you suffocate. It's what right-to-die groups use when helping the terminally ill end their lives. This is clearly the right way to do it, but where do you get one of these bags?"

That would be the next step. Finding the bag.

"Yeah. And a canister of helium."

The body is a heavy thing. When I think about suicide, I think about the tagline from the director's cut of the Coen brothers' first film, *Blood Simple*: "It's very hard, and it takes a long time, to kill a man."

I called my old friend Chellis, who had been rock climbing for five days in Yosemite with her fiancé. She lived in California, south of San Jose and not far from the coast.

Sometimes talking to people on the phone can make you even lonelier. It's like being hungry and smelling a steak.

Chellis asked who I was hanging out with these days, and I realized I hadn't been hanging out with anybody.

She said, "You sound sad. Are you sad?"

And I said, "A little, but not right now. Earlier, maybe." Earlier, of course, was when I was writing about killing myself. The whole situation was just shit.

After thinking about suicide all day, I went out to a club. I put on cartoon-colored tights under my jeans and bicycled into the city with my heels and slip in my backpack. I was supposed to meet Leila at a bar where she was dancing.

Winter had arrived, and the air was sharp. I went over the Williamsburg Bridge, which is peaceful after 10 on a weeknight, and I sliced through the traffic on the Lower East Side. I sent Leila a text saying that I was nearby. She told me not to arrive before 11:15, and to bring her a Red Bull energy drink.

I went into a convenience store and bought a Red Bull, and at exactly 11:15 I entered the club. Leila was wearing boots and knee-high black stockings and high-waisted, lacy underwear. We stood there awkwardly, my fingers occasionally brushing against her leg or ass cheek. The place was empty and dark, with a cement floor. The event organizer was walking around in white face paint and black lipstick and a black sweater. I had my girlie clothes in my bag, but I didn't see any point in putting them on. Leila said she wished she had her equipment—a flogger or a cane. I said, "Why don't you just use your hands? It's the same thing, really."

She introduced me to her boyfriend, and we chatted for a minute about James Franco, who was producing a documentary about Kink.com. I'd introduced Franco to Kink.com, I said; he was also playing me in a movie based on my memoir. It was all true, but I immediately wished I hadn't said it. Leila's boyfriend didn't seem to care. He just walked away. I felt like a comedian doing a set while the audience eats dinner. Leila asked me how old I was, and I told her forty-two, her age inverted. She said I looked good. She said I was so handsome, which was amazing to hear. She smelled like flowers. I was sure she was on some kind of drug, and I hoped it wouldn't wear off too soon, but then she walked away and climbed the small stage and started dancing.

While she danced, I stuffed five dollars into her underwear. She smiled.

I'd been in this situation before. Sometimes it was just a matter of waiting someone out—in this case, her boyfriend. He was so pretty in his torn clothes: tall and skinny, with a flap of blond hair covering his eyes. She was obviously in love with him. It was hard to tell if he cared about her at all. It wasn't going to end well for them, but I was doing fine, and happy to be out of the house.

I got distracted, and when I looked up, Leila was gone. After maybe twenty minutes, I texted her, and she said she was outside; she had to take a phone call from a director.

But I'm a director, I thought, and I'm right here.

Finally she came back. She stumbled slightly, leaning in close to me, and the five dollars I'd stuffed into her underwear fell out. I bent down to pick it up. She didn't notice.

"Hold on," she said, and went to get herself another whiskey. I saw her looking around for something. She stayed gone so long that I put the five dollars in my pocket.

Leila came back and sat next to me. I put my hand on her knee, and we talked about sex. I told her I didn't like sex. She asked if I was a submissive asexual. Yes, I said, but I'm full of desire. It must be hard, she said, to be male and submissive. I shrugged.

At 12:50, I told Leila I was leaving. Her boyfriend was already gone. She hugged me, and I handed her the Red Bull. "It's too late to be drinking Red Bull," I said, and she laughed.

I bicycled home along Second Avenue, past the all-Asian dungeon, and took the Manhattan Bridge instead of the Williamsburg. It was completely empty on the cycling path, and the *whoosh* of cars and trains felt calming. The weather was perfect.

In my apartment I thought about masturbating, but I didn't. I thought about writing down everything that had just happened. I was certain there was meaning in the five dollars I'd given Leila that had come back to me. It was funny but poignant. It also felt like theft. Leila didn't have any money. She was just a kid in her twenties getting high and dancing and enjoying life in the city. She had big plans for herself. She drank too much, but then, everybody has a different tolerance. Maybe she drank just the right amount.

I woke in the morning and started writing. I kept circling around the meaning of the five dollars, coming back to it again and again. In the end maybe it signified nothing.

Having no one to talk to, I went on talking to myself.

"Yesterday I thought, I'm not sad anymore."

How'd that come about?

"It had been almost a week since I'd felt really sad. I thought, I'm not *clinically* sad, but objectively I don't know that my life is worth living. Like, on Tuesday I felt better. And on Wednesday I woke with this headache, but it was OK. I get headaches sometimes. People say they're migraines, but I think they might be sinus related. I've been getting them for years. But then today it was Monday again, and I thought about suicide. It's always like this: first the thought, then the sad feelings. Am I making myself sad, or am I realizing that I was already sad? That's an important distinction."

Do you think this is related to the videos you've been watching? An overexposure to violence?

"I think it might have started there, but I'm not doing that as much anymore. I'm starting to think the videos are just a wall I am trying to maintain against these other thoughts. It's like being in a city under siege: There's Genghis Khan and his army outside the city, and there you are, holed up inside, slowly starving to death as the seasons change. Eventually you just want to open the gates to the Mongol hordes and let them slaughter everybody. It's going to happen eventually."

So you're saying addiction is like a wall surrounding a great city?

"I don't know what addiction is, but I know that what lies beyond it is unspeakable."

Maybe you should go to an NA or AA meeting.

"Yesterday I thought about my housemate from when I was in graduate school. I was shooting heroin in that house, and I overdosed, and the firemen came and carried me down three flights of stairs. When they asked for my parents' contact information, I had just enough presence of mind *not* to tell them how to reach my father. An accidental overdose would only have confirmed everything he wanted to believe about me. He could have told everyone about his rotten junkie son."

You were talking about your housemate.

"Yeah, the guy across the hall: I remember only one conversation I had with him. It was about a cheap sushi place on Clark Street. We both wondered how they served such good sushi so inexpensively. We decided it was because they were doing a high-volume business. I never saw him talk to anyone else. He studied all the time. He was from China, I think. He lived an austere, lonely life. Or maybe none of that is true. Maybe I've just created a story about him. But even if it isn't true of him, there are people who are lonelier than I am—or just as lonely. People whose lives are harder. What's so special about my sadness?"

Why is it so important that your sadness be special?

My father was my age when he quit writing. He went into real estate and did pretty well.

"Writing is hard," he said to me once. "Any idiot can make a million dollars in real estate."

I wanted to talk to him now about his decision to stop writing, but our situations weren't the same: My father never had any success as a writer, even though he was a professional for years. My father wasn't walking away from anything. Still, he had some knowledge of the struggle. He'd lost hope, and then he'd made a change. Which isn't to say he wasn't a miserable person. He had a violent temper, and he would weep like rain. But our parents know something. I'm sure of it.

My father and I hadn't talked in years. The last time I'd seen him, we'd discussed real estate. I didn't want to talk about real estate. I wanted to talk about suicide.

"Yesterday I met Angela and we went to see *Kill the Messenger*, starring Jeremy Renner, about the journalist who uncovered how the CIA smuggled cocaine in order to fund a war in Nicaragua in the 1980s. The whole thing was terrible."

Ronald Reagan was a fucking asshole.

"The worst. After the reporter broke the story, the CIA started a smear campaign against him. He was discredited and never able to work as a journalist again. In 2004 he committed suicide, though by then evidence had been released essentially proving that all of his articles were true. But the movie itself isn't very good. His character is the only real person in it. There's mention of an ex-girlfriend who committed suicide, but nobody else has an interior life, except as it relates to him."

What did you do after the movie?

"We walked down Metropolitan to the water, in front of the new buildings, and we looked across to Manhattan as the sun dipped below the horizon. It was the golden hour and very beautiful. The river might as well have been a painting. The breeze wasn't strong, but it was cold. I told Angela that I'd been sad. 'Don't be sad,' she said, as if it were a choice. She pointed out all of my achievements, which sound better than they are: Like, I've made two movies, but they didn't do very well, and I doubt I could raise money for another. And I've written seven books, but I don't feel capable of an eighth. And, honestly, where are all my friends?"

I'm here.

"You're a figment. You're not even a single person. You represent a variety of people I wish I could talk to. In truth, you're not even that. You're just a stand-in for an antagonist, except real antagonists have their own wants and things they're willing to do to get them."

You're reading too much into everything, treating every molecule of oxygen like a fortune cookie.

"Anyway, Angela and I walked along the water, and after a bit she had to go home. Every Sunday she has dinner with her family. I took my bicycle on the train and went over to a friend's to watch the Giants–Eagles game. They'd made salad and chili and cornbread. It was fine. I stayed until eleven at night and then headed home. I thought I was feeling OK, but on the way I started to think about the suicide bags."

I can't keep having this conversation.

In December I told my therapist I was thinking about suicide.

"How much?" he asked.

"Quite a bit," I said. "But not seriously."

He gave me his cell phone number and told me to use it only in an emergency. Then he asked me to sign a "no-harm agreement" and list a friend I could talk to. "Have you thought about how you would do it?"

"I'd use an exit bag. But I don't know how to get one."

"So you've looked into it."

Yes, I said, but just out of curiosity. The bags weren't readily available. There was one company selling an obvious scam version that wouldn't work.

"Maybe you should go to the hospital," he said.

"No," I said, "I'm feeling better." I'd read about the strain it puts on a therapist when a client becomes suicidal, and I apologized to him for that. Of course he said I didn't have to apologize.

I was hoping he wouldn't have me hospitalized. I felt pretty sure he wouldn't.

And in the days after that, I began to feel much better.

I told my friend Alex I had listed her name on the care document my therapist had asked me to sign. She knew right away what that meant.

"I'm fine," I said. "I just wanted to let you know."

Alex is a good friend but not my closest friend. The others, though, I couldn't use. Ben and Kay and Nick have been through this with me before. And though they would all have said without hesitation that they were willing to go through it again, I didn't think that was quite true. Would anyone ever come out and say, I'm weak from carrying you all these years?

Over the next couple of months I wrote a television pilot about the early days of fetish porn on the Internet. It wasn't particularly good, but it wasn't terrible either. At least I was writing again.

I attended a party in Boerum Hill with a friend who had created a television series that was now in its third season. He'd liked my pilot script and had forwarded it to his manager. I was also with an editor of a literary magazine. When I told her that my publisher wanted to bring out my essay collection, she said what a great press they were. Then I told her how much money they'd offered me.

"You can't sell your work for that little," she said.

I didn't want to talk to her after that. When she decided to leave early, I didn't try to talk her out of it. I stayed at the party and talked to people who were young and ambitious and familiar with the web magazine I'd launched more than five years ago.

I had been doing pretty well for a month or two, but I still felt fragile, like a glass that has been dropped but doesn't appear to be broken.

I've heard that a goal without a plan is just a wish.

Since I started this essay, I have found a relationship of sorts and taken a job with a magazine that some friends started. The difference between a happy ending and an unhappy ending is simply the place you decide to stop telling your story.

When you come out of a depression, it's hard to recognize yourself. You go to sleep one person and wake up someone else. Where did the depression come from? When will it be back?

For almost a year I'd been unable to write much of anything.

I'd barely left my apartment. I'd often gone a week at a time without any human contact other than by phone. When I did write, I could document only the misery. But there's some value in what I produced, simply because it was written while I was inside the tunnel. Anybody who has been through that tunnel knows it's very hard to take a picture in the darkness.

It's the end of winter now. Spring is the best season, no matter where you are.

When you're so depressed you want to die, it's hard to muster the energy to kill yourself. Then, when you start to feel better, you have the energy, but you no longer have the desire. Maybe this is a survival mechanism. Who knows? All I know is I feel better now. I feel quite a bit better.

—New York, 2015

An Interview with My Father

You were born on kind of the tail end of my writing career, when I started investing in real estate in Sheffield. We were doing wonderful business. I would take big old houses, convert them to apartments, and sell them to investors, making a fortune. Then the Labor Party came to power. We couldn't make ends meet, so we decided to go back to America. I went back ahead of you and your mother and sister. In her letters, your mother wrote that whenever you got caught doing something, you would say, "Daddy did it," even though I was thousands of miles away.

I went back to live with my parents in Chicago in a two-bedroom apartment. To save enough money to bring you all over, I went without a car. I had a hard job as a warehouse manager in a place where the elevator didn't work. I'd come home so tired, weeping from overwork, but I was doing it to bring you over because I missed you desperately.

Then, when I had sufficient work, we started over again in America.

I was starting to build my real estate empire again. I bought a three-flat on Albion, where we moved to. Your mother didn't like living with my mother. Two women cannot share a kitchen.

We sold the three-flat, then got a six-flat. Sold that for a profit. I was still working as a driver for the water department. That was a good job. From the thirteen apartments I went to twenty-six apartments. Then I turned those over for a profit.

After I sold the twenty-six apartments, I got apartments on

the South Side and held those for quite a while. We were living on Coyle Avenue, which is where we had all our bad luck.

You were eight and your mother got sick with multiple sclerosis. She laid around quite a lot after that. She had a few little remissions, not much. She just laid there all the time. Broke my fucking heart. I think of your mother every day. I loved her.

At the time, you were complaining that you had to empty her bucket of pee and so forth. Bear in mind, we must have changed her diapers hundreds of times. That's the way it went. You had to look after her when I wasn't home because I had to go look after the real estate. Also, I had to do research into multiple sclerosis and possible therapies for it.

At the same time she was sick, I was getting sick also. I had a prostate condition and I was losing my temper all the time. I would call people names and make personal attacks on my daughter and son, who I loved more than anything in the world. I guess I thought they could take it, but I was mistaken. They were just children, and it was brutal. It made their home such an unpleasant place. Homes are supposed to be a place of refuge, where you come in and feel comfort and at ease and so forth.

We went on like that for five years. I tried to find a therapy that would work for her. There was one that gave her a month's remission and her incontinence a remission that lasted five years, but otherwise nothing helped. And eventually she died. She said, "If this is life, I'd want it. But this is not life." She really wanted to move on to the next world. She was very unhappy, as you know.

I think we were in the living room when I told you your mother had died. I'd already taken her body to the funeral home, I'm pretty sure. Maybe I should have held a service or something, but I don't know. I'm just not a guy who knows what the fuck he's doing all the time. I've always had a hard time with social dynamics and so forth. Death cuts everything off like a knife. I thought I was prepared, but I wasn't.

I took her ashes to England, spread them in the valley, because that's what she told me she wanted. And then I came home. I forget if I was yelling at you or cursing you or some other thing. You were thirteen and just walked out of the house and stayed away all night. That was the first time, probably November. When you came back, I said, "I'm not going to hit you. Our door is always open. If you're not happy here, you can leave."

I still didn't have a clue if there was something wrong with me. It's hard to see the forest for the trees. Looking back on it, I should have said, "Son, you have to spend every night here. That's the law until you're eighteen." I should have made it definite that you can't do anything illegal, can't smoke dope in the house. But I thought, If he's not happy here, there's nothing I can do about it. For the last month you were with me, I made a serious attempt to be calm and quiet and speak nicely to you and so forth. But the damage had been done already, and one month was not sufficient to fix the schism, the weariness that I created in you. You were depressed over your appearance. You matured early, grew a beard when you were eleven or something. I was yelling, calling you names, running you down, making you feel small. You could not find a quiet refuge in our house. And then John was around, who to you seemed like a glamorous figure. All the girls liked him. He was living on the streets, and you wanted to copy him. So you were driven out by me and attracted out by him.

You wanted to lark about, show off to your pals. The drugs probably made you feel good. But of course that's my analysis. I might be wrong. I can't pretend to be objective or omniscient at this late stage. It's funny because I loved you more than anything, but I was crazy.

You turned fourteen on December 3. I was looking back on myself at fourteen. I was basically independent, and I thought, Fourteen is not too young if he wants to live outside. I was not too familiar with the law. You took my ultra-light suitcase, which I'd had for twenty years or so, and took your belongings and went.

Other parents make all the right decisions.

I started seeing Kit in the spring before your mother died, or the winter. She was in a soccer class I was teaching. She came over and met your mother and loaned her a book. Kit and your mother were great friends. Kit and I were aligned boyfriend–girlfriend or whatever, but your mother had no objections. She said she hoped I would marry Kit when she passed on.

I can't say it was a bad thing. De facto I was a single parent with a disabled adult and two children. Your mother was not a wife in any way. I had to carry her everywhere. I didn't have any ill will for that. I still don't. I'm just saying. I was a single parent. That's the truth of the matter.

I forget when we got married, but Kit wanted to live in Evanston, and I had no objection. Coyle had been bad luck for us. I found a house that was a good investment, but I had to sell the house on Coyle. It was a very difficult time to sell. I did not expect to profit. In the meantime I'm running my other buildings on the South Side, trying to keep them up.

In August of that year, we closed on our new house and moved. I didn't know where the fuck you were. At one point I ran into you coming out of Roger's grandparents', and you ran from me. I wanted to bring you to our new house on Michigan, but you wouldn't even talk to me. The grandparents called the police. I tried to explain that you were a runaway and I wanted to talk to you and I was your dad. But the police got in the way. They wouldn't let me talk to you. And you insisted you didn't want to talk to me.

Any time we tried to bring you in, there was an objection on your part. You didn't want to live with Kit. You didn't want to live with your uncle. You made it clear you didn't want to hang out with me. You had no curiosity about where we lived, what we were doing. I left a notice of our new address with the post office. You say that's not good enough for a fourteen-year-old. Well, of course not, but I didn't know where you were, and even if I did, would I want to give you our new address? It's hard to say. I didn't have firm ideas about it. I went through the motions anyway.

So I'm trying to sell this house on Coyle, and after a hard day's work, I come in there and I find you put out a cigarette on the windowsill. You've been in there. I'm trying to sell this goddamn house, and I'm a janitor. I'm not giving a three-bedroom house to a fourteen-year-old boy. I went down to the video-game parlor, and I warned you not to go in that house anymore. I was not rich. I'm not rich. And I needed the money. You didn't want to live with us when I was there, and now that it's empty, you want to make yourself at home. Well, it's not acceptable. And one Sunday I came in and you were there, and that's when I pulled you up and you started swinging on me. I restrained you with the force necessary to make the arrest that I was taught in the sheriff's department. Did I hit you? I don't know. Maybe. I don't think anybody's ever seen you with a bruise or a cut lip. I restrained you, no question, as forcefully as I had to. And if I did it angrily, it's because I was upset. When you tell people I shaved your head, that's fair enough, I guess. Everybody else said I shaved your head. I was just so angry I couldn't get control of the situation. I was just crazy crazy crazy. Afterward I came upon you sitting on a bus bench and asked you what your plans were, and you said, "Well, I guess I'll just commit suicide." I had to go to work or something, and I didn't know what the hell to do about that. I do know that if you had committed suicide, I would have been haunted for the rest of my life. I would have never recovered. So fortunately you didn't.

That was not the first time I shaved your head. That was probably the second time. The first was when you had been telling people at school that I was abusive. That must have been spring, when you were out on the street with John. But you were still going to school. They asked me to come to school, and you were called into the meeting, and I said, "Tell these people, How is it you mean I am abusive?" And you shook your head, leaving the impression that there was sexual abuse of some kind. Anyway, that's the way I thought.

I was so angry you had told people I was an abusive dad that I brought you home and hit you and cut your hair. You had hair down your back. I wish I had never hit you and cut your hair. I can't begin to tell you what a terrible memory that is for me. Afterward you were sitting in the bathtub crying.

That's the first time I cut your hair. I still have pictures of it. But that haircut was not quite so close. The second time I did it to stop you from going into that house. I'm still unhappy about it. I probably shouldn't say these things, but I'm going to anyway, because I might not have much time left in this world. If you want it, I'm going to be cooperative. The hell with it. I'm not worried about how I look anymore. Doesn't matter.

One time I handcuffed you. I had been under tremendous pressure from people who said I should have you institutionalized. So you were living on the street with John. I must have taken you from the video-game parlor. People were saying you should be locked up, given to a psychologist, but I had a feeling that would last only so long as we had insurance to cover it. I had a feeling it was a racket. I brought you home, handcuffed you to a pipe for about thirty minutes while I tried to figure in my own mind, reach a decision, about what I wanted to do. Fortunately, after thirty minutes, I decided, Fuck all those people. I took the handcuffs off and said, "You go and do whatever you want."

Now it's August of that same year, and the state takes you to Read Mental Health Center. They must have picked you up the next day, after I caught you sleeping in the house. I'm notified one way or another and invited to Read. I made appointments with the therapists, and they always stood me up. Always. Those cocksuckers. And I never once saw the psychologist who wrote up the report on us. DCFS* never had anyone visit us in our home. Nobody ever saw us together, period. To say we were dysfunctional is just made up out of their heads. I never even had an interview with anybody. It's just bullshit they made up.

I went to see you a few times, but you didn't want me, and the state tried to take you. You obviously wanted to go with the state, and at some point I said, OK, the state wants him, the state can have him.

I don't know when you ran away from Read or whatever. By November you were totally lost to me. Finally, some social worker slipped or was a good enough guy and told me that you were in a home on the South Side. The home was near my building. I brought you over to the building and gave you some work painting. John also did some work.

That December we started to get friendly again, or not friendly, but I knew where to find you. We were in association. Then you went to JCB Home on Campbell. A nice home, as far as I could tell. It wasn't too crowded. You said you once asked to live with me on Michigan. I believe you, but I can't recall it offhand. It was probably good you lived on Campbell. We were separate. I still had my moods. I was still yelling at the little kids that Kit and me were having.

Rich kids go away to boarding schools. Prince Charles was not raised by his own mother. So it's not terrible you were in a home and I was in another house nearby. Nobody bothered you on Campbell. Nobody yelled. They gave you free room and board. I was still a crazy person. From my standpoint it turned out to be ideal, because we could become friends. And we did too. We

---

* Department of Children and Family Services

started going to poetry readings together. We went to the No Exit Café. Even after you left JCB, we were still together quite a lot. So I think we were friendly. There was always a little bit of weariness because I didn't quite understand you. I was always afraid I'd lose track of you. That was my biggest fear.

Then at some point you went to college, then graduate school. We continued to be friendly over the years. We'd have coffee together.

Victoria says you dance like me. Dancing and writing, that's what we do in our family. I used to be really good before I lost my legs. Real athletic. I wish I could have played an instrument. I've got a good voice for singing. Could have been a rock star.

—*Chicago, 2009*

Neil Elliott died of a heart attack on September 4, 2015.

A Place
in This
World

Now a row of log cabins, now a road with no cars,
now a field waiting for the season to return.

Jimmy Wallet Is Buried Alive

Here is a photograph, undated. Jimmy Wallet is seated, his face turned, the sharp lines of his chin and jaw like an alligator that doesn't bite. He's terrifically handsome, with a boyish nose and cheeks, a sly smile, a little patch of beard below his lip, long black dreadlocks past his shoulders. His oldest daughter, Jasmine, sits next to him. People say she should be a model. Hannah is sprawled across Jimmy's lap, looking at the camera, laughing, Jimmy's hand covering her stomach. Behind him are his two younger girls, Raven and Paloma, and his wife, Mechelle. Raven looks up to her mother, who is turned and kissing the baby, her lips against Paloma's mouth and nose. It's a perfect picture, and soon it will be all over the news.

Jimmy Wallet is in motion now. He's walking to the store. He has a loping, lazy, long-legged walk, arms bouncing near his waist. He's wearing baggy jeans, a red sweatshirt, and a sleeve-less leather vest. The day is serene. Jimmy breathes deep, smells the Pacific, the sage from the hillside, the jasmine from the yard. When he left Mechelle, she was cleaning up the house, packing boxes, organizing the children's things. There've been tornado warnings, and Mechelle is worried they'll have to evacuate. The three younger girls were on the sofa when he left. Jasmine is in Ventura with her boyfriend. Mechelle told him on his way out, "I need some milk crates or something so we can organize."

So he's looking for milk crates, and he plans to buy ice cream for his little girls. Some people say Jimmy gives his children too much ice cream, but he doesn't care. Every good father knows that children need ice cream. He takes the opportunity to light a cigarette. He's been trying to quit, but not today. The cigarette tastes good. If he takes his time, he'll be able to have another one. He checks out the sky, which is mottled in patches of soft blue. It's been raining for weeks. Dark clouds linger over the ocean and beyond the avocado trees looming six hundred feet high on the edge of the cliff abutting La Conchita, a tiny town of 250 people between Ventura and Santa Barbara. Maybe the good weather is coming back. Maybe he'll take the girls to look for arrowheads later. This area once belonged to the Chumash, and when rain washes down the hillsides, there are secret pockets where you can find artifacts if you know where to look.

It's January 10, and the world looks surreal. The sun dips in and out of shadow, casting a filmic light across the town. The lawns are wet and look like they've been brushed with glaze. The damp air carries a cool salt breeze. In the distance Jimmy can just make out the Channel Islands and the oil tankers sitting on the water, all of it hooded in fog. And there are no birds. Today all the birds are gone.

Jimmy reaches the store and throws his arms in the air. CLOSED. It's the only place in town to get liquor, gas, ice cream, the basics. The store is located at the entrance to La Conchita, a precarious left turn off the 101 Highway heading south. The gas pumps are on Surfside, the first of the town's two streets that run parallel to the highway. Jimmy and his family live on Santa Barbara, one of eleven short streets that crosshatch the town. The house is just below Rincon, the higher of the two long streets, closer to the cliff. Not quite against it. A block up the hill is a row of houses destroyed in a landslide ten years ago. Those houses still stand, never rebuilt, the roofs collapsed, beams poking from hills of dirt.

"Hey, Gator," says Brie. "What are you doing?"

Her hands are tucked in her sweat jacket, her hood down. She lives with her boyfriend, Isaiah, in the same house as Jimmy, upstairs in the crow's nest. Isaiah's father, Charlie, built the room, all four walls made of windows. Brie's twin sister, Annie, lives with her boyfriend, Griffin, in an Airstream out back. Brie stands with Isaiah and his brother, Orion, and a half dozen others.

"It's closed," Jimmy says, jerking his thumb toward the gas station and extracting another cigarette. He gives Brie a look that says: Can you believe it? But then he remembers why everything seems so strange: the highway is closed, which explains the store being closed. The 101 straps against La Conchita like a tight belt, a four-lane concrete barrier between the town and the beach. Normally, the white noise from the thousands of cars rushing between Santa Barbara County and Los Angeles is as constant as a sky without seasons. You live in La Conchita, you learn to ignore the highway. You look west and you see the big blue ocean and maybe some caps from the turning surf, but you never even see the cars.

But today there are no cars at all, and *that* gets Jimmy's attention. No cars, no birds. At two points north of town, water accumulated on the upslope faster than it could drain out; the mud funnelled down from the canyons and poured over the railroad tracks, onto the highway. Geologists call it a soil slip, a debris flow no deeper than the roots of plants. Still, the slush is two to four feet high in some places. More than fifty vehicles, including a passenger bus, are stranded. A UPS truck is buried to its window. A Honda minivan that had been floating toward a drainage ditch has been lassoed, its side-view mirror looped with twine and staked to the ground. Three command transports from the fire department are there, including the specialized swift-water rescue team. The swift-water guys wear wet suits and carry a Zodiac in case they decide to do a water evacuation.

In La Conchita it's like a silent holiday. There are children out, playing in the road. It's Monday; those children should be in school. But no one's driving anywhere today. People who would normally be at work in Santa Barbara or Ventura are milling around, riding bicycles, sitting on their porches. A few La Conchitans have crawled through the four-foot drainage tunnel that runs beneath the highway and connects the town to the beach. A group of maybe fifty is down by the tracks, rubbernecking at the rescue site. But by 1:15, after more than six hours, the operation is coming to a close. The stranded motorists have been helped through the mud to a waiting sheriff's bus and transported to a shelter. The Ventura police department is clearing the cars.

A news crew covering the rescue resets its cameras just down the street and starts doing man-on-the-street interviews. A helicopter passes overhead, swooping up the slope and disappearing behind the ridge. Jimmy cups his cigarette in his hand. He's stalling now. One more cigarette and he'll go home.

"We should have dinner on the beach later," someone suggests to Jimmy as he slides the cigarette between his lips. Dinner on the beach—why not?

A child throws a ball high in the air. An artist who lives three doors down from Jimmy leaves pasta to boil for her two children and stands on her porch, staring across the empty highway to the water.

"Look," someone calls. "There's dirt coming down."

Jimmy and Mechelle have been in La Conchita only three months. They met at Ventura High School when they were both fifteen and have been almost inseparable ever since. It was adolescent infatuation that never faded. They married just out of high school and had their first child at twenty-one. They're thirty-eight now and still in love.

But the previous year had been hard. Jimmy suffered a back injury on a construction job and has been out of work. He didn't belong to a union; there was no insurance, no benefits. There was no money, and the family had nowhere to live. Mechelle left him, took the girls and moved in with her grandmother. Jimmy moved in with friends in Pierpont, sleeping on couches. He stayed out late, got in trouble with the police.

Somewhere in that time Jimmy hit bottom. He had no work. He'd lost his wife and his children. It seemed like every morning he woke on a different couch. He called the best man he knew: Charlie Womack. He asked if he and Mechelle and his daughters could maybe come stay with Charlie and his family in La Conchita. Charlie's answer: "What took you so long?" Jimmy laughed, relieved, and said he'd just been waiting for the right time. To make room for the Wallets, Charlie moved himself into the teepee in the yard. Then he got Jimmy back to work in his construction business.

But that's Charlie: the biggest heart in Ventura County. Fifty years old, tall and rangy, a musician and a DJ, a legend in the surfing community for his contributions to the design of the five-finned Bonzer board (and for being the first surfer to ride it), Charlie moved into his house in La Conchita seven years ago and right away set about making it his own. He laid flagstone tile in the kitchen and mixed concrete with orange stain for the counters. He installed a six-burner stove with a hood and a beer fridge outside. He built decks surrounding the house, tended guava trees, brought in a wooden hot tub from 1972. His children— Orion, twenty-six, Isaiah, twenty-five, and Tessa, fourteen—live with him and revere him possibly even more than his friends do.

Also notable on Charlie's property is a lime-green bus, a beast of a vehicle with yellow and red stripes and a string of dancing zebras. There's a gigantic deck on top—the best place in La Conchita to watch the sunset—and a recording studio inside.

This year Charlie intends to take the bus to Burning Man. Jimmy and Charlie sit out there at night singing songs, Jimmy on bass, Charlie playing guitar. Isaiah joins them sometimes, and some of the neighbors too. Nobody ever tells them to keep it down. Twelve people live on Charlie's property, sometimes more. Charlie's nickname is Llama, like the monks, and they call themselves the Llama Tribe. Brie does most of the cooking on Charlie's giant stove. She loves to cook: roast chicken for Charlie and Isaiah, homemade marshmallows for the kids. Mechelle helps. Christina Kennedy from across the street often brings the food.

That's La Conchita. Some people down the road in Ventura say it's nothing but weirdos and hippies, but that isn't entirely true. The town has an undeniably loose vibe, but most people have jobs: lawyers, electricians, schoolteachers, surfers, engineers, musicians. There's no crime; you can leave your door open at night. Mike Bell, the unofficial town mayor, a retired safety coordinator for the Los Angeles Department of Water and Power, carts a wagon down the streets and hands out margaritas. People call him Margarita Mike, and he's friends with everybody.

Jimmy and Mechelle are happy here. They fit in. When Mechelle's not homeschooling her girls, she makes vegan cakes that she sells all over the county, or silk-and-velvet eye rests filled with flaxseed and lavender, to help people sleep at night. Hannah sews, like her mother, makes clothes for her Barbie dolls. Two-year-old Paloma is learning the drums. She's decided to marry Isaiah but tells Brie she can still live with them.

With Charlie's help, Jimmy has put his life back together in La Conchita. The two of them build frame houses together, pouring concrete for the base, laying foundation, putting up walls. When Jimmy isn't working, he lifts Hannah on his shoulders and cruises town with his little girls, Raven carrying a longboard that's twice as long as she is. Everybody waves at them; it's like being on parade. Jimmy calls it Never-Never Land, a paradise for his children.

Beach parties, surfing, community. Sunsets like lipstick on cotton. Whales from your bedroom window. The last place in Southern California a poor man can live with a view of the ocean.

Monday, 1:20 p.m. First a snap, then a pop of white smoke. The landslide takes eight seconds.

The soaked hillside detaches from the scarp, breaking apart as it tumbles at speeds up to thirty feet per second, dust like smoke above a viscous four-hundred-thousand-ton slab of earth. A collective gasp escapes from the crowd watching the rescue operation. The mud moves like a cement river, makes noises like airplanes piercing the sound barrier, runs like thick soup down the slope, into the retaining wall. The flow rams the wall and shoots thirty feet in the air before blasting through the structure's center, simultaneously diverting south toward Jimmy's family. Power lines slap together; a flash crackles above the mud.

"Look out!" yells John Morgan.

Kyle Larson had been loading some things into his car on Rincon. He hears Morgan's scream and takes off down the hill.

Greg Ray, who had been helping Kyle, dives between two cars. A trailer spins over the top of him and flattens the vehicles down to the wheels.

Jimmy and Isaiah sprint toward their home.

The mud fills houses, and the houses pop like water balloons. The slide carries trailers and cars as easily as paper. Below the surface, the trapped vehicles operate as blades, clearing the land of human debris. Phone poles buckle and fall. Everything lifts from, then sinks into, the ground, like fruit in a blender. Countertops crash through garages, dressers spin over shingles, cars ride upside down across a tide of broken windows and floorboards. Jimmy and Isaiah keep running.

A bus turns over just yards before Jimmy. Mud cakes its fender. Earth plasters its bent grille. Streets disappear beneath mud twenty and thirty feet deep. A roof collapses. That house belongs to Diane Hart, Jimmy's neighbor. Isaiah and Jimmy scramble up the caved-in roof, onto the top of the mound.

"No, no, no."

Firemen rush up from the highway, their heavy jackets flapping at their knees. Jimmy digs into the earth, searching for his family. He reaches as far as he can, but it's almost impossible to get his hands in. As quickly as it fell, the mound has hardened into a dense mass, heavy as granite. His hands fill with splinters and stones as he pulls rocks and beams from the wreckage. Nothing is where it was before.

An eight-hundred-foot shelf of land, pushed up from the ocean eons ago and pounded with near-record rain for two weeks. Most of the rain ran off, leaving the front of the mountain dry and hard beneath its thin, wet surface. But farther up the hill, the water seeped through fractures left from the '95 slide and soaked behind the scarp like a garden hose filling a swimming pool, raising the groundwater level, saturating a weak layer of clay beneath the mountain. When the mountain failed, it was like a battering ram on ball bearings, the fluid clay deep below the surface carrying the heavy, dry earth above it. It was only a matter of time—the young rocks, the weak material, the near-vertical face, the steep scarp left from 1995, pressured from the ocean like a rug pushed across a hardwood floor, a tug-of-war between tectonics and gravity, the long folds of earth struggling toward their angle of repose.

Search-and-rescue teams are dispatched from Moorpark and L.A. County, the hulls of their vehicles filled with aluminum shoring, video equipment with collapsible necks, gas sensors, wedged cribbing, sound-monitoring devices. The site is quickly divided into disaster zones; round-the-clock support is initiated. Natural gas leaks from pipes twisted like licorice while gasoline spills from vehicles ripped open like sardine cans.

Isaiah hears moaning inside the pile and reaches through the wood, splinters digging into his forearm. Isabel Vasquez, who was visiting a friend, who doesn't even *live* here, is pinned beneath an armoire, trapped against an exterior wall. She grasps Isaiah's hand.

Others are saved too. Diane Hart, a nurse, buried in a closet stuffed with pillows she had made to protect herself from tornados. Kyle Larson, a photography student, moments ahead of the mountain, survives only because of John Morgan's scream and the thick traction of his heavy fishing boots. Greg Ray, a retired Disney animator, was wedged between the battered trailers and cars in a space no larger than a coffin. He's pulled from his tomb after three hours.

There are early casualties: Tony Alvis, who led tours on horseback and was said to have known the Los Padres National Forest better than any man alive. Christina Kennedy, who had been putting the final touches on a BMW she had rebuilt in her front yard. Vanessa Bryson, who was supposed to have left town today for a new job at an AIDS hospital in Seattle. And John Morgan, a quiet but friendly man who'd tended the grounds at the naval yard for thirty years and who allowed homeless men to park on his property.

Jimmy digs until he is exhausted, hair matted and soaked with sweat, his arms burning, folded over his knees, working above cracked timber on the perimeter, then throwing a piece of roofing at one of the many camera crews that have descended on the tragedy. "If you're not going to dig," he shouts, "then go away."

The sheriffs seal off the area. Late at night, Jimmy thinks he hears his daughters crying. Monitors are inserted into the ground, electronic ears listening for whispers of heartbeat. Nothing. The geologists say if it rains again the mountain will move, and at eleven the rain returns. Arc lights set above the mounds blur the stars, blending day into night.

Jimmy brings six friends from Ventura, and they help him dig all night. Early in the morning, he drives Jasmine back to her boyfriend's place, and when he returns to La Conchita, he's arrested trying to re-enter the area. He's forced down the road in handcuffs, crying, "My family is in there. I've been digging for two days!" The battalion chief on duty decides to allow Jimmy to continue with the rescue efforts. When a sheriff warns him that it's dangerous, Jimmy replies that he doesn't care if he dies.

On the second day, prison crews arrive in neon jumpsuits. Heavy equipment rolls in. Bulldozers and tractors scratch the mound, searching for spaces. When a void is found, the machinery stops and the prisoners operate in human chains, extracting buckets of earth. Isaiah and Jimmy are allowed to work alongside them. Residents who have left La Conchita to sleep with relatives and friends in Santa Barbara and Ventura sneak back into town along a trail from Rincon Beach.

Thirty hours after the mudslide, hope is all but gone. The birds have returned, but how did they know? The last rescue was made more than twenty hours ago. Dogs troll the earth, snouts pressed into the ground. These are not rescue dogs. They're trained to smell cadavers. But the air reeks mostly of mineral deposits ripped from the cliff.

Late Tuesday, Jimmy finds Raven's shoe. Just before he went out for ice cream, he had tucked a jacket over his youngest, placed his bass guitar next to her, and given her a book. Raven liked to feel she had her own space. She was different from his other daughters, louder. Blond hair and blue eyes, like her mother's father. When she was born she wasn't breathing and had to be given mouth-to-mouth resuscitation. She'd been talking ever since.

No man should survive both his wife and children. Jimmy lies in the street and prays.

In the end, there are ten rescues and ten fatalities. Jimmy and Isaiah are credited with saving two lives. Charlie Womack is found dead a few minutes before eleven p.m on Monday night. Mechelle Wallet is found late Tuesday night and identified by Jimmy at two a.m. Wednesday morning, mud caked on her lips and in her long black hair, her pale skin like plaster.

Hannah, Raven, and Paloma are the last victims to be found. They are next to each other beneath the purple couch they had been sitting on, exactly as Jimmy said they would be. The bodies are brought to the gas station, which had been turned first into a triage center and now into a morgue. Jimmy leans in to smell his children. He presses his nose against their faces. They smell like the dirt and rock of the landscape around them.

There's a ranch house in Carpinteria, California, five miles north of La Conchita on the 101. Jimmy Wallet lives here with Isaiah and Brie, Annie and Griffin. Brie's fourteen-year-old brother, Justin, lives in the house, and so does Charlie's youngest daughter, Tessa, also fourteen. There's a room for Jasmine too. Jimmy hopes she'll move in—she's only sixteen, after all—but for now she chooses to stay with her boyfriend in Ventura. It's a small house for the survivors of the Llama Tribe, with one bathroom, a small kitchen, and a small yard in the front where they can see the green mountains in the distance. They've planted flowers in the front yard. A friend of the family has given them four months of rent for free. The owners are planning on tearing it down within the year.

Brie has lost her taste for cooking, so they eat out a lot. When they sit in restaurants, people point and whisper: Are those the mudslide survivors? So terrible. They don't fit in here. Carpinteria is a quiet, affluent community with shopping malls and quaint restaurants. It's a nice place, but you wouldn't sit on your porch playing music late at night. The engraved wooden sign that greeted visitors to Charlie Womack's house—MUSIC IS LOVE—now sits in their living room, which is also a bedroom.

By ten p.m. every night the house is dark. Early in the morning, someone takes Tessa and Justin to school. Twenty-five-year-old Isaiah is the father now, head of the household, responsible for the children and keeping the tribe together. He's good at it, kind of like his dad was, but a little more practical. He's returned to working on a construction truck and is fighting to keep custody of his little sister. He watches over Tessa's schoolwork, and her grades improve from Ds and Fs to As and Bs. He teases her, and she reminds him he's not supposed to do that anymore, he's the adult now. "Oh yeah," he says, messing her hair. "That's right."

A lumberyard nearby has offered to donate wood. Isaiah hopes they can persuade someone to give them land so they can build their own house. They dream of moving back near the mountain.

Jimmy's hair is turning gray. The walls of his room are painted earth red and covered with Buddhist drawings and pictures of his children. There are sticks of willow on the ceiling, which are supposed to keep bad spirits away. He's been reading books on death and dying, books of poetry, books on spirituality: *Highest Yoga Tantra, Tara the Feminine Divine, The Book of Buddhas.* He's trying to homeschool himself the way he and Mechelle taught their children. He wants to write poetry but can't seem to get it on the page. Instead he speaks his poems to his friends and asks them to remember.

He wears his grief on his outside. It's hard sometimes to breathe. He searches for other people who have suffered a similar loss but can't find anybody. His mind floats back to one day in late December. The children were asleep. He and Mechelle were lying in bed, watching footage of the tsunami in Asia, feeling awful for the people on the other side of the world watching their kids float away. They held each other for comfort and they cried. At the time, the rains were just getting started in La Conchita.

One night Jimmy almost gets in a fight at a bar in Ventura when a drunk off-duty fireman tells him he wouldn't help the people in La Conchita, because they're living at their own peril. "I would help you," Jimmy replies, a friend tugging at his arm, trying to keep the two men separated. "I would die for any person in this bar."

Some people say Jimmy's doing well, all things considered. As good as can be expected. Some say he hasn't changed at all, he's still spiritual, he's still full of love. He tries to reassure the people around him. But Isaiah worries about him, talks about taking him somewhere so he can get his head straight. He'd like to take Jimmy to Hawaii or Mexico for a little while but can't imagine how.

Jimmy doesn't remember where he goes during the day; he doesn't have an answer for the question of how he spends his nights. He leaves Carpinteria for days at a time. He says everything just blends together since the mudslide. He knows he visits Jasmine. And he knows he spends time on the hill.

One night in mid-March, Jimmy pulls the covers and rises from his bed. He gets in his car, gets on the 101, and heads south. The air is cool. He passes an oil plant, its chimney shooting a flame into the night. As he rounds Rincon Beach, a blinking yellow light announces the intersection ahead. He pulls into La Conchita.

More than half the residents have returned, despite warnings. Several days after the mudslide, a journalist asked one of the residents why he lived in La Conchita; the man just pointed west to the Pacific. The reporters are gone now; the houses are dark. There is only the sound of birds and the ocean and the steady whine of cars below. A fence encircles the disaster area, which covers about a quarter mile. Inside the fence, buttressing the mountain behind it, hills of mud and debris rise twice as high as the roofline.

Jimmy lifts the fence at its edge, squats close to the ground, one hand in the dirt, and slips inside. On top of the nearest mound are two yellow-and-red sections of his daughter's playhouse, held in place by rocks. At the bottom of the piles are toys: a rubber ball, a plastic doll, a torn-up football. The fence is covered in flowers and decorated with red ribbon that spells HAPPY BIRTHDAY, PALOMA. Brie and Isaiah tied it there on March 15, which would have been her third birthday.

This is where he feels most comfortable, where everything was going so well, near his children, the mountain at his back, the ocean spread out in front of him. He comes here almost every night.

Early spring, early morning, and there are already a half dozen surfers in the water. The waves are six to eight feet and seem to run perpendicular to the shore because of the shape of the cove. The water crosses itself, with one set of waves rolling toward the harsh rock outcropping as another set moves in a broad arc toward the beach. The land below the highway in this part of Ventura County curves at nearly ninety degrees, creating a perfect break, provided you don't stray too far from the cove and get washed across the rocks. Just beyond the pier is the beach attached to La Conchita, the small path beneath the highway its only access point.

A blanket of dark clouds is gathering. The rain may be coming back. A young girl, no older than ten, her hair loose and free, catches wave after wave in the cove. She cuts through the other surfers, riding the water's sharp edges away from the shore, toward the islands in the distance. She disappears in a tunnel of bright water, then appears again, the ocean bubbly white beneath her. Finally, the wave curls into itself, and the child is flicked from her board like an ant from a lunch table. No match for nature, she spreads her arms wide, a long, thin band attached to her ankle. The board tilts up, dives into the surf. The girl disappears, then emerges moments later.

—Ventura, California, 2005

The New New Middle East

We're seeing the birth pangs of a new Middle East.
—Condoleezza Rice

*We should go to the Arabs with sticks in hand and
we should beat them on the heads; we should
beat them and beat them and beat them until
they stop hating us.*
—Israeli taxi driver, *Arab and Jew: Wounded
Spirits in a Promised Land* by David K. Shipler

1

Moments ago they closed a street in Jerusalem. The police came and unspooled red tape and wire as cars backed up Jaffa Road. They wore heavy vests and carried big guns, but they were laughing. Two storekeepers plugged their ears. There was a small explosion. Someone had left a bag sitting in Ben Yehuda Plaza. This is one part of Jerusalem.

At Mike's Place in West Jerusalem, the tables are outside and a breeze cuts through the courtyard. I play pool with my friend Maimon, who lives here now with his wife and child. We met at a ski resort eight years ago. I was hitchhiking under a full moon and the white glow of the mountaintops when Maimon stopped to give me a ride. I got a job bartending at the top of the gondola lift, and Maimon taught snowboarding. When we weren't working, we zipped down the mountains. Those were endless days, when the only thing that mattered was the depth of the snow.

But that was Colorado, and this is where Jesus died and Mohammed rose to heaven and the Jewish Temple stood for a thousand years, leaving nothing but a retaining wall, where the Hasidim knock the brims of their hats and kiss the bricks and leave notes and prayers for their god. The capital of a nation at war.

Maimon tells me a story about his time in the Israeli military, before we met.

"I was in the infantry," he says. "We were in Gaza, and they were launching mortars at us. We saw where they were setting up. They were in an orphanage. I fired at them, but it was night. I shot with an M60, which is a nineteen-pound machine gun that fires five hundred and fifty rounds per minute. Do you understand what I'm saying? I had coordinates, but I couldn't see anything, and I was firing on an orphanage."

From the bar we head to the Western Wall, where I leave a note on behalf of a friend and kiss the wall. I should perhaps make my own wish for the war to end, but I'm not a believer. We are close to the Via Dolorosa, where Jesus fell carrying the cross he would be nailed to, and we can see the gold dome of the al-Aqsa Mosque. The old city, with its ancient walls and cobbled roads and armies of devout singing and muttering in the dark, is perhaps the most beautiful place on earth. I will go to Gaza soon, twenty-eight miles long and surrounded by an electric fence. All I need is a press card.

When I go to get that card, they don't want to give it to me. The press woman says, "What is the *Believer*? I have never heard of your magazine."

"The *Believer* is a big magazine in America," I say. She stares blankly at me. "Maybe not that big. It's a prestige publication." I

ask if she would like a copy, and she looks through me with hatred. Finally I prevail upon her.

When I leave I say, "Have a nice day." I kind of want to ask her on
a date. I don't know anybody in Israel except Maimon. She says,
"I will not have a nice day. Fourteen Israelis have just been killed
in Lebanon."

A Hezbollah spokesman says the soldiers were "burned alive
in their tanks on our land."

2

It's quiet in the town of Kiryat Shmona, or it's very loud. This is
the largest town in northern Israel, and when the rockets land,
the ground shakes. Then nothing. Everything is very tense.
Sometimes the rockets are incoming, but usually Israel fires west
to the border. The town is practically empty. The stores are closed
except for one, and I stop there and have a beer with a clerk who is
watching Keanu Reeves in *Speed*.

Many of the residents here have moved to a camp on the
beach fifteen miles north of Gaza. The Israeli army is taking
more casualties than they expected. The Lebanese are faring
much worse. In 2000, the Israeli army pulled out of Lebanon unilaterally after eighteen years of occupation. In 2005, they also
pulled out of Gaza. They're building a wall to block out the West
Bank and stealing some land in the process while creating new
"facts on the ground" as the settlements grow. The leaders of
Israel say they don't negotiate with terrorists, but it looks like
you have to negotiate with your enemies. A nation can't negotiate with itself.

I walk at night, watching for the flash of tank muzzles. I see a
woman smoking a cigarette, her dog nearby. She doesn't pay any
attention to the missiles falling. A handful of lights is on in the

windows. A couple of cars parked, the rest of the spaces empty. I stay in the military hotel near the bus station, and a soldier steals my computer while I sleep.

The next day I ride in an armored car with Uwe, a large, bald, ruthlessly ambitious press photographer from United Press International. We drive past a field where a missile has struck, leaving a crater and a small fire. There are tanks, troop carriers, D9 demolition vehicles. The D9s are horrific machines with giant steel shovels on the front and thick, round bars surrounding their torso in a cage. All of it built upon the frame of a tank.

We come upon a military installation, but the officers won't let us inside. The entire north, they say, is a closed military zone.

"The north's not closed," says Uwe. "They're just not letting us in. They don't know what they are doing. They don't give a shit about us. The other night the army publicists showed us the bodies of Hezbollah fighters. They were wrapped in plastic bags, and they had their guns next to them. They were like hunting rifles. I said, 'Hey, these guys are giving you trouble? C'mon.'"

We cross another gate, into the border town of Avivim. There is a Lebanese village half a mile away, but it is empty. I want to cross the border. "No way, man. Everything is booby-trapped." I ask Uwe for his jacket and helmet, but he just laughs, spins the car around. We can see the minaret of the mosque in the rear window. I feel like we could go over there. Talk to people.

"I'm too young to die," Uwe says. "And I love my life."

We continue through the rocky countryside. It's beautiful here, but also very hard. Past artillery and the occasional ambulance. This is the land of kibbutzim, Israeli idealism, communal farms. We wind up the hills along the border.

We pass another missile smoldering in the earth. We hear explosions, then pass the bushes just set to burn. We can't get back inside Avivim, so we take a dirt road through the back. There are giant tank guns pointing at us when we exit the woods, but the gunners just smile and wave. Some of the soldiers rest on the ground, heads leaning against their knees. Soon, though, we are turned around, and it takes an hour to get back because all the roads are closed. Then there is small-arms fire coming from the Lebanese side. Then machine-gun fire from the bluff above us. We stop, surrounded. The cannon bursts are continuous now. There is another village across the valley floor, and there's fire and smoke there. The sky is blue and purple.

We are the only car in the road. It's nearly dusk. I ask myself what I am doing, but I know what I am doing. I'm heading into danger, hoping to understand conflict and war and the price of land. Maimon said I was crazy to come here, but he's already served two tours in the Israeli military.

Finally we pull out carefully, back the way we came. There is a great cloud of smoke from behind a Lebanese hill. Massive gunfire, shelling. We drive to a plateau and park and get out. There's a TV crew there. Soon there are more photographers watching the smoke and the movements.

"They're bombing a new village," Uwe says.

Two helicopters hover in the sky above us. The choppers drop flares like flaming shit from pigeons, hoping to distract the Lebanese missiles by drawing them to the heat. Then we see a plane in the distance and realize that is what the helicopters are protecting.

The plane, everyone thinks, is carrying the new bunker-buster bombs delivered express by the Americans. Now all the cameras point to the sky.

In the distance two more villages are burning. Or maybe they are the same ones. "You see all the helicopters and missiles," Uwe says. "I think they are really flattening those places."

The hills are filled with *whir! bang!* and *boom!* But here in the Upper Galilee, way up high in the strategic position, it is hard to tell the human story contained in that smoke: the families huddling in shelters, trapped children burning to death, others crushed by beams, cut to ribbons by exploding windows, entire families incinerated. Four hundred Lebanese have been killed so far, sixteen hundred wounded.

This part of Israel, the rocky sliver of land between Syria and Lebanon, has always known fighting. This is where the Syrian army crossed in 1973 and where the PLO attacked from its fiefdom in southern Lebanon prior to the Israeli invasion in 1982. In 1970, a school bus in Avivim was attacked. Nine children and three adults were killed, and nineteen children were permanently crippled. In 1974, three members of the Popular Front for the Liberation of Palestine snuck into Kiryat Shmona with directions to take hostages. Instead they entered a housing complex and killed eighteen residents inside.

We leave the plateau, again through woods. Up higher we come upon a tank unit. Two soldiers load the gun, another soldier rests on the hood. "You have to serve in the military here, so you appreciate your country," the soldier tells me. "We're doing a good thing, and we're going to change everything."

"Do you think so?"

"I hope so. We lost five soldiers out of our group. My friend lost both of his legs, and we got him out in the tank. There are only fifty soldiers in my unit, so to lose five is a lot. The guys that are dead, I want to visit their families because I know them. But I can't because we are at war right now."

"A soldier stole my computer this morning," I tell him. "I was staying in the military hotel. It was plugged in, sitting on top of the refrigerator. Somebody came in and stole it while I was sleeping."

"A soldier is like anyone," he tells me. "A soldier also steals."

Two days later Uwe and I get stuck in an apple orchard on the Lebanese border while waiting for Israeli troops to return. I decide to leave and walk out onto an empty road, closed by a checkpoint nearly three miles away. I realize I am walking alone on the border and I could be shot and there would be no return fire. It's my first taste of the fear.

On the day when at least twenty-eight are killed in an Israeli shelling of an apartment building in Qana, Lebanon, a hundred missiles rain on Kiryat Shmona. Four missiles fall near our hotel, and a reporter from *Haaretz* is taken to the hospital with shrapnel wounds. He had been interviewing someone whose house had been bombed when another bomb fell on the building next door. The firefighters around Kiryat Shmona are out spraying the fields. There are six injuries in Kiryat Shmona, and property is destroyed, but nobody dies, because the town is nearly empty and those who stayed kept to the shelters.

The Lebanese who died were in shelters as well. They thought they were safe. But Israeli bombs are stronger and Lebanese buildings are weaker, and the building collapsed and everybody perished and the pictures are all of dead babies covered in dirt and rock.

As the Israelis push deeper into Lebanon, the Lebanese missile fire focuses on the Upper Galilee, the northernmost point of the country. Shaba Farms is here, just a few kilometers from the city. According to the United Nations, Shaba Farms belongs to Syria, and Israel keeps it, waiting for a treaty. But the Lebanese say it belongs to them, and Hezbollah says it will fight until every inch of Lebanon is liberated. So when Israel withdrew unilaterally in 2000, Israel kept Shaba Farms, which it had taken from Syria in 1967. There are people who joke that the war with Lebanon is over three acres and a goat. There are others who say that if Israel had pulled out of Lebanon when the PLO left for Tunis in 1982, there would be no Hezbollah. But nobody knows.

At a kibbutz near the border, there is a pond and a small field filled with deer. Soldiers back from Lebanon lie around the water, clips removed, rifles slung loosely over their shoulders. There are signs warning people to beware of the animals. A deer was born two weeks ago. They named him Katyusha, after the rocket.

When the first rockets fell near the hotel this morning, it felt like the walls were going to break. We ran to the porch, saw the blackened field, the smoke rising, fire on the hills, and also smoke coming from where we couldn't see to the west.

Safed is a holy city, supposedly founded by a son of Noah and certainly dating back to the Romans. It's the center of Jewish kabbalism. Madonna was here recently, swimming in the purifying waters. Like the Upper Galilee, Safed is mostly empty. There is still a guard at the coffee factory, but the coffee isn't being processed. He shows me where the missile came through the roof into the third floor. "I would have been standing right there, but I was on my break. I was playing sudoku."

From the roof of the factory, we can see the scorched hillside near the hospital. The hospital's windows are broken, and tops of buildings are smashed in places. I meet a man who has just returned from southern Israel, where the rockets can't reach. He talks to me about the fear. "You're playing Russian roulette," he says, "walking in the streets." He says they have a safe room in their house. "You shouldn't be here. If you hear a whistle, find a wall and stand behind it. If you feel something, be careful."

I meet Jonas, an American Jew who has decided against leaving. His child brings me a twisted piece of rocket that landed nearby. Jonas wants to know what my angle is.

"I'm anti-victim," I tell him. He invites me into his house, and we talk about fear. He says the rockets started falling on the same day the walls of Jerusalem were breached in ancient times. He says today is the anniversary of the death of a famous scholar and that normally there would be ten thousand people here.

"We were fasting, and when we broke the fast, we set up a table outside, and a rocket came and exploded when it touched the top of a tree only twenty feet away. The tree saved my life. You don't know," he says. "You don't know if it will land here or in the valley or in Haifa. We seem safe sitting here, but we're not safe.

"Listen," he says. "There was a woman who was six months pregnant, but she went into labor early. She goes to the hospital. When she comes home, her house has been destroyed. You see. It was a miracle."

Jonas invites me to stay, but I don't. Jonas says, "They want to push us into the sea. They will wait, and wait . . ."

There is danger everywhere, but it is nothing compared with the images broadcast from Lebanon, entire cities reduced to piles of rock. Some argue that what matters is who started it. Others say it is a disproportionate response. Everybody wants to feel safe, but that isn't what people are fighting for. Jonas thought the Arabs and the Jews would always be at war. I mentioned Jordan and Egypt, but he didn't think that counted for much.

Back to Tel Aviv. The beach in the evening is warm and peaceful. People here don't really feel what is happening closer to the border. This is the secular heart of the country, where people drink and dance and swim in the ocean and nearly everyone speaks English. There are sex shops and parties, and nothing seems to have slowed down. I sit at Mike's Place. Maimon meets me when he gets off work. And we are too late when the tow truck comes and snatches Maimon's car. It takes only seconds for the truck's bars to slide beneath the chassis and hoist the car in the air. Maimon screams at the police officer, pulling on his own hair.

"You have another job for me?" the officer asks. "I'll do something else."

3

The day before I'm supposed to go to Gaza, I ask an Orthodox Jew at a bus stop where I can find a synagogue. He introduces himself as Michael, and he invites me to go with him to the Western Wall; it happens to be the anniversary of the destruction of the temple. Michael hasn't shaved in three weeks. Jews are supposed to suffer to help them remember. Some people put dirt in their shoes.

On the way we stop at a demonstration protesting the forced removal of the settlers from the Gaza Strip. They wave orange flags, and some have orange strips tied to the ends of rifles.

Michael tells me I'm not half-Jewish. "That's like being half-pregnant. If your mother's not Jewish, then you're not Jewish." I feel rejected. "C'mon," Michael says. "I didn't invent these laws. Do you think I don't want to eat pork?"

We talk about the temple and the al-Aqsa Mosque. Michael says when the temple is rebuilt, we'll all live in peace. "We all believe in one God," Michael says.

"But you'd have to remove the mosque to rebuild the temple," I say. "Where Mohammed rose to heaven."

"No. We would just move it. It's not even their holiest place. It's only their third-holiest place. They pray with their backs to the temple."

"It's hard to imagine the Islamic world being OK with moving al-Aqsa," I say.

"It's hard to imagine a wolf and a lamb," Michael replies.

I think about Michael on my way into Gaza. *When the temple is rebuilt, there will be peace on earth.* It's not something I believe, but religious extremism has risen on all sides of the Israeli conflict. I think about Maimon, whom I saw later that night. We were in the Old City, filled with Orthodox Jews mourning the temple.

We met an old friend of his on her way to the wall. Maimon whispered to me after she passed, "She's not Orthodox. She used to fuck." Maimon got his papers the other day. He's being called up for military service, even though he's forty years old.

Most people aren't thinking about the war in Gaza, since everyone is focused on the war in the north with Lebanon. But 175 Palestinians were killed in Gaza in the past forty days.

Gaza is a hard concept to grasp without going there. It's barely twenty-five miles long and four miles wide. There are 1.4 million people, making it the mostly densely populated place on earth. One million of them are refugees from the Israeli War of Independence, in 1948, or what Arabs refer to as al-Nakba, or the Disaster. Of those, 860,000 still depend on the United Nations for food. They are citizens of no country. The crossing to Egypt has been closed. The port for imports and exports has been closed. The crossing to Israel has been closed. All of Gaza is surrounded by an electric fence. Journalists and humanitarian aid workers are the only ones who can get in and out.

At the border there are three buses. America and Germany are taking their few citizens from Gaza to the Jordanian border. Everyone with a foreign passport is leaving. They laugh at me for going in. "We should kidnap you," one of them says.

I walk a long, quiet tunnel built for processing thousands. A large gate opens at the end, and I step into a chamber. The gate closes behind me, and another opens. Sunlight scatters inside through holes in the roof. I pass a restroom covered by razor wire. Then I hear Arabic music and step into the Gaza Strip.

Ashraf is there to meet me. "You look good!" he says. "You took out your earrings, and your haircut makes you look like an Arab."

"That's because an Arab cut my hair," I explain.

"Don't tell anyone you're American," he says. "People here don't like America anymore."

We pass a destroyed bridge over a ravine that will flood when the rains come in the winter, houses reduced to rubble. There are some cars, but there are also carts driven by horses and mules. Posters of men surrounded by guns are taped to all the buildings. The men have died recently and are celebrated as martyrs. We pass the settlements the Israelis left just a year ago and destroyed on their way out. We pass a distillation pump donated by Italy, crowded with Palestinians waiting with jugs for the taps.

"Nobody can drink Gaza water," Ashraf says.

It's been five years since I last visited Gaza, and at the time, it seemed like things couldn't possibly get worse. But things can always get worse. Gaza is the graveyard of optimism.

If you ask when the current round of destruction began, the Gazans will say it began with the death of the Ghalia family, killed by Israeli artillery while on the beach near the Erez Crossing, where I came in. Israel denied that its ordnance was responsible, but human-rights groups have displayed fragments of a 155mm Israeli artillery shell. Many Israelis believe that only militants are killed in the fighting. They don't believe in collateral damage, but war is nothing if not mistakes. The image of the surviving child, Huda, captured the world's imagination for a few days and the imagination of the Gazans for much longer.

The Israelis say the conflict started with the election of Hamas, whose militia continues to launch Qassam rockets across the border. The rockets are small, but they do damage, they terrorize the population, and eight Israelis have died. The Israelis believed that when they unilaterally left the Gaza settlements, the militants would cease their attacks. But they were wrong, and this has infuriated the Israeli public, who feel like they have given something and gotten nothing in return. But the Gazans, who don't control their ports or crossings and have no international representation, don't see what they have to be so excited about.

At the hospital in Rafa, the head surgeon sleeps on a mat on the floor. "There were nine martyrs today," he says, trying to wake up, lighting a cigarette.

"There were also twenty-three wounded," the surgeon says. "Today I amputated four extremities. We fear there will be more martyrs because of infection. We suspect the IDF [Israel Defense Forces] attacks again tonight. Always we fear at night."

I notice that even the hospital walls are covered with posters of the men who have been killed.

Mosheer Al Masry is thirty years old, a member of Parliament, and the Hamas spokesman in Gaza. We meet in his apartment in Beit Lahia, a particularly hard-hit suburb just north of Gaza City. There is a sitting room in the front and a curtain to prevent us from seeing the women in the rest of the house. He is well dressed, with a nicely trimmed beard.

Mosheer tells me it is just the Israeli media that says Hamas refuses to recognize Israel, and that Hamas has always been willing to negotiate. This is a lie, but I let it pass. He tells me, "America should correct the policies of its government. They will be more welcome in the world." He's just a kid with a beard, I think. I mention that the charter of Hamas calls for the destruction of Israel. Mosheer waves his hand and smiles. He offers me an orange soda.

At night I sit on the Mediterranean, on the patio of the Al Deira Hotel, where the richest people in Gaza meet. They wear Western clothes. Women sit at tables with uncovered heads. There is no alcohol, since the last bar, the UN Beach Club, was burned to the ground, less than a year ago. Among the patrons is a smattering of foreign press documenting the tragedy playing out, second-stringers covering a forgotten war since the hostilities with Lebanon to the north. There are almost no foreign-aid workers left in Gaza, and there are fewer than a hundred people sipping strawberry juice and smoking narghile pipes, talking and listening to the sea.

With its beautiful beaches, Gaza was once thought of as a potential tourist attraction, but all the hotels are empty except for Al Deira, which costs eighty dollars a night. Ashraf offered to let me stay in his apartment for free, but the water didn't work, and there are only six to eight hours of electricity. I was hoping to save some money, since the Israeli military stole my computer, but when Ashraf told me I would need to keep away from the windows and open the door only if I heard my name, I decided I would stay in the hotel.

I sit with Hamada, the Gazan head of a UN organization. His office was destroyed several days ago during a riot that erupted to protest the UN response in Lebanon. "The people you see here," he says, "they are here every night." It's like the deck of the *Titanic* after the last lifeboat had gone.

Hamada's foreign counterpart has left Gaza already. I tell him I met a sick man earlier who was dying and had been waiting more than a month to leave for Egypt and get care. We talk about the impossibility of a targeted assassination. "There are four thousand people per square kilometer. There's no such thing as a targeted killing in that dense of a population." We talk about the crowding and poverty, twenty people living in one room with no basic sanitary conditions. The sewage running through the streets of the refugee camps, where the majority of people live.

"The main problem of Gaza," he says, "is access."

We talk about the import-export zone, which has been closed. There was a project to grow vegetables in the hothouses bought for the Gazans from the settlers by the World Trade Organization. After the settlers left, it looked like the project would be a success. But then, when it was time to export the vegetables, the port was closed, so the tomatoes sat on the dock, going rotten.

We talk about the phone calls. In the past months, the IDF has taken to calling people and telling them their homes are going to be destroyed. Often in less than ten minutes. The problem is that this has led to prank calls. "My neighbor got a phone call," Hamada says. "'We're going to bomb your house.' We didn't go home for three days; there was no way to verify."

Then there are the sonic booms. Ehud Olmert has vowed that as long as Qassam rockets are coming from Gaza, the Gazans will not sleep. When there are no troops in Gaza, planes fly over, breaking the sound barrier, releasing noises like giant bombs.

To illustrate the animosity between the Palestinians and the Israelis, Hamada tells me about the Beit Lahia wastewater plant. "The plant contains two million cubic meters of raw sewage in a lagoon. The plant is not working because of the lack of electricity. To make matters worse, the Israelis bomb the lagoon to prevent absorption. If something isn't done soon, the plant will overflow. If the plant overflows, it will flood an entire neighborhood. The flood will cover four hundred fifty houses. The only thing to do at that point will be to push the sewage into the sea, which will kill all the fish."

I imagine four hundred fifty houses filled with two stories of shit. I wish they served alcohol here. But when we talk about solutions, Hamada disappoints me. He talks about the right of return, which is the idea that all the refugees from the 1948 war should be allowed to return to Israel. It's the kind of idea suggested by people who are not looking for a solution. Most of the homes and communities they would return to have long ceased to exist. Hamada says that Israel provokes all the intifadas and that the Qassam rockets are just firecrackers, when in fact the Qassams have destroyed homes and claimed lives. More important, the Qassams are a provocation.

The problem here is that a Gazan intellectual with a good job with the United Nations cannot see the part his own people must play in any solution. History, Israel, the United Nations, the Arab nations, particularly Egypt, have created a welfare state and an echo chamber in a cage. This echo chamber is oblivious to news coming in from the networks and the Internet. People don't trust information from the outside world because most people don't know anybody from the outside. Here, in response to the seizure of a Palestinian militant in Jericho, rioters destroyed the British Council, where people could get job training and borrow books. In response to the war in Lebanon, they destroy UN offices, even though the UN is the only real employer left and is responsible for feeding and housing more than half the population. Hamada doesn't see the role the Palestinians have played in their own misery, the kidnapping of the soldier, the election of Hamas. In this way he's no different from most of the Israelis I've met, who blame all their troubles on Arabs. I let Hamada pay for my juice.

I lie awake in the middle of the forgotten war. There is some gunfire in the streets, or perhaps just fireworks from a nearby wedding. I watch CNN, and the current death statistics filter across the bottom of the screen, followed by a doping scandal in the Tour de France. I ask myself, If I were stuck in this cage and unable to make contact with the rest of the world, what would I do?

The second most important man in Gaza, after the leader of Hamas, is John Ging, head of the Gazan United Nation Relief and Works Agency. He's the only person in Gaza willing to criticize the Hamas government. But then, his office is giant and air-conditioned, and he can leave when he wants to. Ging says:

> The tragedy is, after all this time, we still feed eight hundred sixty thousand refugees in the strip. With the recent incursions we've added a hundred thousand to our rolls. Donor assistance has been cut off since March, when the Palestinian Authority, under Hamas control, didn't meet

donor requirements. There are no garbage trucks to pick up waste, for example. We're at the relief end, providing the very basics. We have four schools at the Jabalia Camp that we've now filled with fifteen hundred people seeking shelter from the Israeli military. This is the first time the Israelis have cut off power, so things are much worse. The sense of imprisonment is heightened. Anybody with the option to get out is already gone. What the Palestinians don't understand, when they launch their rockets at Israel, is that the damage might not be the same, but the fear is the same. People get distracted by the magnitude of force. Israel should rein in its military. The PA, which is run by Hamas, has the responsibility to stop the Qassam rockets. Hamas can form a legitimate government, but there cannot be a separate military wing that exists outside of the government. They also have to recognize Israel and recognize existing agreements. Over the years there've been so many false starts. We see a flicker of hope, most recently the settlements leaving. We thought we would now move on to economic development. But it didn't happen.

I visit a school filled with families whose homes have recently been destroyed. I see the schools and the rooms filled with mats. Each room sleeps roughly fifty people, with separate rooms for women and men. Many have lost homes near the Israeli incursion zone, the homes destroyed for strategic reasons. They tell me about the phone calls—parents running with their children, and eight minutes later, their house is destroyed. One family explains how their house was bombed two weeks prior. The only grown-ups in this family are women and a very old man. Their brother was killed over a month ago. "And then they shot the cow," they tell me.

"What?"

"After the Israelis bombed the house, they shot our cow."

Before I leave Gaza, Ashraf shows me the universities. There are two, al-Azhar University and the Islamic University. Al-Azhar University was founded by Fatah. The Islamic University is at least unofficially affiliated with Hamas. Al-Azhar is decrepit, the buildings in disrepair despite the fact that it is newer. The Islamic University is pristine and orderly. This is why Hamas is in power in Gaza. Under Fatah, a tenth of the population was employed by the government, but the police wouldn't stop the most basic of crimes. But Hamas runs clinics, and its security forces are effective. Islam offers structure in a place that knows only war. Hamas did not come to power because of its position on Israel. The idea that Hamas can be forced from power by starving Gaza is false. Hamas is the power here; it controls the message. There is no one else to negotiate with.

4

My first night back in Jerusalem, I go to a gay bar with an Orthodox rabbi and others who have arrived in Jerusalem for the gay-pride week that is coming up. He asks me what I think of the idea that Islam doesn't work because it was founded on success, while Judaism and Christianity are founded on failure. "Well, it's not true," I say. "At least for the Shiites. Anyway, I don't think you're getting at the heart of the problem."

I remember Ashraf just back from the mosque. I asked him what he heard, and Ashraf responded that the preaching concerned America and the evil use of American power. I remember the destroyed buildings, and Ashraf pointing and laughing. "American made! You make very good bombs. Look, they go through six floors. It's amazing."

The rabbi and I watch the transvestite burlesque.

"I love this," he says.

"I wouldn't mind doing that," I say. The tall black woman is lip-synching "I Will Survive."

"Are you good with makeup?"

"No," I reply. "And I twitch. My mascara would be everywhere. But I do feel most comfortable in a dress and heels."

We watch the show and dance until midnight, when the rabbi leaves. He has to be up early for an interfaith meeting. He's hoping to spread tolerance and acceptance for gays in the religious community.

On my last day in Israel, Maimon and I meet back in Tel Aviv. I want to talk to him about the third side of the conflict, the one simmering in the West Bank, the land between Jordan and Israel. Israel has built a security barrier separating East Jerusalem from Ramallah and Bethlehem, cutting off 40 percent of the West Bank economy. I want to talk about the giant settlements like Ma'ale Adumim, built between East Jerusalem and Ramallah, with forty thousand residents already and forty thousand more expected in the next few years. I want to tell him I visited the Tomb of the Patriarchs, where Abraham is buried, father of the Arabs and the Jews, and how you could feel the pain of the conflict simmering in the streets of Hebron and the small settlement there and in the square in Kiryat Arba, named in honor of Baruch Goldstein, who in 1994 slaughtered twenty-nine Muslims while they were praying. It's a small country, but these are all places Maimon has never been. I want to talk about the conflict and the history and how hard it is keep the story together when there are so many threads.

But when Maimon sits down, he looks very serious.

"I ordered a pitcher," I say.

"Good idea," he says. Then he starts to cry.

I get up and hug him. He'll be reporting soon, going off to fight in Lebanon or maybe Gaza or to staff a checkpoint in the West Bank.

"Oh God," he says again and again and again. "I just got the call. My cousin was killed in Lebanon." Other people, waiting outside for their meals, look away. A man passes the bar carrying a surfboard. Maimon doesn't have the details yet, just that it happened more than twenty-four hours ago and they haven't been able to recover the body yet.

We sit in the restaurant for as long as we can. The sea is so close. The only real border, where the land ends. Maimon makes a joke, then starts crying again. "Lebanon," he says.

At the airport terminal, as I am getting ready to leave, Maimon says, "Remember Colorado?"

"Sure."

"All we did was snowboard all the time."

"Yeah."

"Remember when you got fired?" he asks.

"I had stolen a snowboard from Vail Resorts."

"Yeah."

We try to laugh, but it's hard.

—Tel Aviv, 2006

California Superpredator

1

Sometimes he hears voices. Often, they are just whispers. On December 2, 1999, it's the voice of David Foster. David is thirty-five and one of the most feared people in the neighborhood. Alonza is walking home from school, wearing a light-blue shirt. "Hey," David says. "Come here."

Alonza runs, but the man catches him, sliding his heavy arms below Alonza's thin arms, locking the boy into a full nelson. "Why you wearing blue?" David says. "You a Crip?" David's gang pours from the alley, surrounding the child. Some of the gangsters are children too, younger than Alonza. Three are girls. They kick Alonza's legs, hit him with elbows, smack him in the head with a forty-ounce beer bottle. Alonza falls to the ground. A foot stamps his face; the voices are screams. He digs at the cement, the rocks catching under his fingernails, lost in the bodies chanting "Bloods, Bloods, Bloods."[1]

Fifteen-year-old Alonza Rydell Thomas lives in Bakersfield, in the sprawling desert of the Central Valley. The city is expanding. It's now the thirteenth largest in California, with 221,000 people. They're putting up pitch roofs faster than stoplights. People keep arriving from Los Angeles, snatching up the cheap houses. There

---

1. *The People vs. David Foster*, SC214A.

are parks on the map, but the parks aren't built yet. There are parts of Bakersfield with every chain restaurant you can imagine but no post office and no library. Drive half an hour just to send your mail. And there's a ghetto not far from downtown, in the eye of the sprawl, filled with low, dark bungalows, marked by their lack of air-conditioning. It's like living in an oven.

He's six foot three, thin as straw. He has a child's shoulders, a child's smile. He's knobby and loose. There'd be something almost handsome about him if he weren't so awkward; there's something wrong with his head. He's not a bad kid; he doesn't get in trouble. He's not in a gang. His record is as clean as an upscale restaurant. His mother is a schoolteacher. Her name is Janice, but everybody calls her by her last name, Venus. His daddy lives in San Diego. He stayed with his father for a year when he was twelve, but his father got rough and Janice had to call the police, bring him back home. He has two brothers, normal as can be.

Janice and Alonza see David Foster stopped by the police. Janice tells the police that he is the man who beat up her son. Alonza appears in court to testify against David Foster. Foster is sentenced to thirteen years for a series of offenses and parole violations.

February 2000, desert winter. A note comes from school—Alonza has been failing his classes. In response his mother takes his money, four dollars. Alonza thinks his mother doesn't love him anymore. He's never had a keen understanding of consequences.

He sits near the tracks east of Truxtun Avenue, just down from Kern County Superior Court. The slow-moving train passes overhead, while the underpass tunnels beneath the rails. Alonza swings just for a second, long fingers gripping the steel-gray container, hauling himself into the empty car, traveling north toward Sacramento. He has become a statistic, one of two million American children who run away every year.

Two weeks later Alonza returns. He stands at the door of his own home, but the door is locked. It's late at night, and he thinks his mother has locked him out. She says later she just didn't hear him. He disappears into the city.

Alonza meets a man known as Baby Boy. Now they are partners. The man gives him food, beats him, molests him. Tells Alonza if he wants to go home, he'll have to rob a store. At least, that's what Alonza says later, after he's been sitting in a jail cell for a couple of weeks. No way to know if it's true. But there is some evidence to support it.

March 21, 2000, 6:20 p.m., the Fastrip convenience store on Mt. Vernon, right out there where those new houses are being built and the streetlights don't work. A quiet neighborhood; never any crime. The store sells gasoline, alcohol, and snacks. Alonza Thomas ties a scarf behind the back of his neck as the sun falls behind the mountains, leaving a hazy twilight for the moon. The gun is a .22, the second most stolen gun after the .38 and the third most popular for criminals, accounting for 16 percent of all crimes involving guns.[2] Alonza could close his fist around the gun and it would disappear.

He enters through the side door, wearing latex gloves, holding the firearm sideways. He waves the gun at the three men behind the counter.

For a moment the three men think it is some kind of joke, the scarf and the latex gloves and the way he holds the gun.

"Give me the money," Alonza says. He doesn't look behind him. He doesn't seem afraid. He walks straight to the counter and presses the gun against Nassri's chest, and the men no longer think it is a joke.

"You want the money?" Nassri Jaber states calmly. Nassri is the

---

2. James D. Wright, Peter H. Rossi, and Kathleen Daly, *Under the Gun: Weapons, Crime, and Violence in America* (New York: Aldine, 1983).

owner of the Fastrip. He isn't supposed to be in tonight. "If you want the money, I'll give you the money." He opens the register, takes the bills out, hundreds of singles, also fives, tens, twenties. Maybe $300. But he misses a twenty, and Alonza sees it.

"Money, money!" Alonza says, getting irritated. The men are becoming frightened. "I thought he was going to kill me," Nassri says later in his deposition. The owner opens the register and gives Alonza the last twenty. There are no customers. It's time for Alonza to leave, but he doesn't. There is something wrong with him. His eyes are like glass.

Alonza slides the gun from Nassri's shoulder. "Open the safe," he says. The safe is on the floor beneath the register. Nassri bends toward the countertop. Alonza isn't paying attention. Ali Salah, the clerk, grabs Alonza's wrist and yanks him forward. "He made me do it!" Alonza cries, a stack of jerkies tumbling to the floor.

Othimi, the other clerk, hops the counter. The gun goes off. A *pop* like a paper bag, followed by smoke. Nassri grasps the phone. "My employee has been shot," he says to the police. But he's wrong. The gun discharged, but no one was hurt. The bullet has lodged in the Formica, where it will stay.

Othimi hits Alonza in the head. The men struggle through the store, bottles and snacks falling from the shelves. It takes several minutes to subdue the boy. He seems stronger than his size. He bucks. His gun sits on the tile. The two clerks pin the delinquent. Nassri places his own gun, a .40 Glock, against Alonza's temple, warns him to stop moving. Eight squad cars, a helicopter, and an ambulance are on their way. Nassri's so angry, he wants to shoot. Alonza's scarf is yanked from his face. Nassri thinks to himself, He's just a child.

2

What Alonza Thomas doesn't know is that two weeks before he walked into the Fastrip food mart holding a revolver sideways and demanding money, 62 percent of California voters approved the Gang Violence and Juvenile Crime Prevention Act, also known as the Pete Wilson Initiative, or Proposition 21.

It's not an easy bill to understand. The initiative runs forty-five pages, contains twenty-four new priors, and amends dozens of existing provisions, rewriting the California criminal code. Lawyers claim it takes three full days to go through, *and* a law degree. Proposition 21 revises specific crimes for both adults and juveniles, changes available probation options, reduces confidentiality protections for juvenile suspects, reduces the threshold for felony vandalism to $400 from $20,000, and adds significant penalties for gang-related crimes for adults and juveniles—including the death penalty for gang-related murder.

Most significantly, Proposition 21 changes the process of trying children as adults. The most serious juvenile felons, the rapists and murderers, were almost always already tried as adults before the passage of Proposition 21.[3] Less serious but still violent crimes, like the armed robbery committed by Alonza, *could* be tried in adult court with a judge's approval prior to Proposition 21 but usually weren't.[4] Those cases can now be filed directly in adult court at the whim of a prosecutor. This process, known as discretionary direct filing, is a favorite of the California District Attorneys Association, a group closely tied to the bill. But voters don't know about discretionary direct filing. They think they're voting against gang violence. They think they're voting

---

3. Prior to the passage of Proposition 21, juveniles who committed the most serious crimes were presumed to be tried as adults. If there was a reason to try someone as a child, the burden was on the defense. It was exceedingly rare for a young murderer to be tried as a child. Proposition 21 now mandates that all serious offenders be tried as adults, allowing no room for mitigating circumstances.

4. Proposition 21 also added crimes for which a child could be tried as an adult. In 2003, the last year for which data is available, there were several children tried in adult court for vandalism.

to allow children to be tried as adults. They don't know that children can already be tried as adults. They don't know that what they are really voting for is the removal of judicial oversight. The bill won't save money. The removal of oversight is assumed to cost hundreds of millions of dollars.

Politicians have rarely lost elections for being too tough on crime. This is particularly true following the upsurge in youth crime between 1987 and 1993. In 1995, John Dilulio, a professor at Princeton, coined the term "juvenile superpredator." The juvenile superpredators, according to Dilulio, are "radically impulsive, brutally remorseless youngsters, including ever more preteenage boys, who murder, assault, rape, rob, burglarize, deal deadly drugs, join gun-toting gangs and create serious communal disorders."[5] Dilulio predicts that the number of American superpredators will swell in coming years if immediate action is not taken. "What we need," he says, "are more churches and more jails."

The superpredator burns through criminology like a lit butt in a bale of cotton. Academics like James Q. Wilson begin warning of a modern plague of youth crime. "Thirty thousand more young muggers, killers, and thieves . . . ," states Wilson. "Get ready." But the plague never arrives. In 1994, juvenile crime begins to drop. In 1997, crime has leveled off to pre-1987 statistics. In 1999, Wilson concedes, "So far [the rise in youth crime] clearly hasn't happened. This is a good indication of what little all of us know about criminology."

Nonetheless, former governor Pete Wilson, in a short editorial supporting Proposition 21, quotes James Q. Wilson,[6] predicting

---

5. William J. Bennett, John J. Dilulio, Jr., and John P. Walters, *Body Count: Moral Poverty . . . and How to Win America's War Against Crime and Drugs* (New York: Simon and Schuster, 1996).
6. Professor Wilson, now at Pepperdine, did not return multiple requests to clarify whether he ever supported Proposition 21 and if he supports it now.

that in coming years, "California murders are most likely to be committed by a seventeen-year-old. This is a tragedy for the victims and their loved ones, but also for those youthful perpetrators who, despite preventive measures and intervention by state and local public agencies, are so hardened and remorseless that they cannot be turned from violence. It is they from whom society must be protected."[7]

It costs a lot of money to get a complicated initiative on the ballot. A Nevada casino and a Texas auto insurance company each give $10,000 to the signature-gathering campaign. Chevron donates $25,000, Pacific Gas and Electric gives $50,000. Another $50,000 comes from Unocal. Unocal's spokesman says, "We have a strong interest in youth." Chevron spokesman Mike Marcy says his company contributed "at then-Governor Wilson's request."[8]

The campaign to get the initiative on the ballot raises three-quarters of a million dollars. But when Wilson leaves office and his presidential campaign founders, the corporate donors disappear. The measure sits on the docket like a weed.

Proposition 21 takes effect on March 8, 2000. Alonza Thomas is the first child in Kern County tried as an adult under the new rules for discretionary direct filing. The juvenile superpredator has come to life, the unredeemable child. In March 2001, Alonza is sentenced to thirteen years in adult prison for armed robbery.[9]

---

7. In 2003, the last year for which data is available, twenty kids are tried in adult court for petty theft, sixteen for alcohol-related offenses, ten for disturbing the peace, and eight for vandalism.
8. *Mother Jones*, January/February 2000.
9. According to several attorneys consulted for this article, if tried as a juvenile, Alonza would most likely have spent three to six years in juvenile detention.

3

There are flowers in the garden and well-manicured lawns at the Tehachapi state prison, a level IV adult correctional facility in the Kern County Valley. Upon arrival, in September 2001, following six months in the California Youth Authority, Alonza is placed in a small isolation cell, usually reserved for punishing problem inmates. He's given a series of medical, psychological, and educational tests. He is fed in his cell, released only a few hours a week for showers and exercise. While children are being processed, they don't go to school. Processing usually takes two to three months but sometimes more.[10]

Alonza and the others are confined to maximum security in the new Youthful Offender Program, in a separate, beige wing with barbed-wire fences, where they are prepared for the mainline. There are two small concrete outdoor exercise areas originally designed for adult administrative segregation inmates. The children do not have access to the counseling and rehabilitative programs available to juveniles committed in the California Youth Authority. They spend their time in small groups in a windowless dayroom the size of a king-size bed. They sleep two to a room, have access to television and radio unless they are under administrative segregation. School is canceled because of fog, because of lack of space, because only five of the eight teacher positions are filled. Rules are strict and enforced. A third of the juvenile inmates in the adult prison are in administrative segregation at any time. Children in administrative segregation do not go to school.[11]

---

10. Report of the Inspector General, State of California, Tehachapi Youthful Offender Program.
11. When Alonza enters corrections, he has finished the tenth grade. He makes no progress toward a high-school degree after entering prison.

Alonza is transferred for short-term psychiatric treatment six times, where he is placed on medication, stabilized, then returned.

Janice parks in the dirt lot set in back of the Tehachapi campus. She is with her two other children, twelve-year-old Phillip and seventeen-year-old Patrick. They wait in the entry for their names to be called. They are searched, their hair is checked, gone over with a wand, processed through a metal detector. Their hands are stamped. They wait for a bus. Thirty people board the bus and drive two minutes to another check-in facility, where they are searched again. They walk through a glass corridor, through an outdoor pathway, and into a building, where they take a staircase down. Here is the visitors' area, sectioned off to the left for visiting juveniles. Janice and her sons sit at a table as high as their knees. Games are available, checkers, backgammon. When Alonza arrives, his face is swollen like a ripe plum, eyes yellow with purple lids, cheeks red and bruised.

"Who did this to you?" she asks. His eyes are so large, he can barely open them. He sounds like he's speaking through a sponge.

"Don't worry, Mom," he says. "It's taken care of." Janice doesn't believe him. She calls the prison to complain.

In 2003, scandal rocks the juvenile unit at Tehachapi. Many of the children are mentally disturbed. The weeks and months in isolation cells exacerbate their condition. Alonza attempts suicide while in Tehachapi. In March, a delegation of clergy visits and finds a boy kept in a solitary cell in the infirmary, where seriously deranged adult inmates scream at him and expose themselves on the other side of the door's small window. Children tried as adults in Los Angeles County are held during trial at the Men's Central Jail, kept in isolation 23.5 hours a day. In May, two juveniles at Men's Central attempt to commit suicide. In

July, Francis Ray, a seventeen-year-old youth offender serving a three-year sentence for second-degree robbery, hangs himself after four months in an isolation cell at Tehachapi. State Senator Gloria Romero orders an investigation.

When Janice calls Tehachapi to check on her son in August 2003, an officer tells her, "He won't be coming back here."[12]

One of the arguments made in favor of placing juveniles in adult facilities is that they are a drain on resources better used on children for whom rehabilitation is considered a possibility. The report from the inspector general strongly recommends a reversal of this policy. Tehachapi's special juvenile unit is closed in July 2004.

4

It's 110 degrees at ten in the morning in the Antelope Valley, the sky a deep, empty blue. A short, muscular prisoner named Vince Crittendon approaches the fence wearing a sleeveless top and blue jeans and fingerless gloves for weight lifting.[13] He's been in prison for twenty years on a thirty-to-life sentence for robbery and murder. He calls to a man in a shiny brown shirt and muted tie.

The man Vince calls to is Ken Lewis, assistant to the warden. Vince wants to talk about his son. He hasn't seen him since the boy was five. He tells Ken his son is next door, on the C unit, serving seven years for something involving "drugs or guns." He wants to see the child. Ken explains it probably won't be possible. Vince's son is in a special-needs section and is not allowed to mix with prisoners from other units.

---

12. According to prison files held at Lancaster, Alonza's last day at Tehachapi was July 31, 2003.

13. Vince Crittendon, prisoner #C-57138, requested that his information be made public.

"OK," Vince says, nodding. "I just thought I could get through to him. Help him understand."

They're in the honor yard, a special unit reserved for well-disciplined prisoners serving life with little chance of parole. To be in the honor yard, a prisoner must spend five years incarcerated without incident, have no active gang affiliation, express willingness to program with inmates of any race, and be drug-free.

The honor yard is the highlight of California State Prison–Los Angeles County, in Lancaster. It's the only honor yard in the state. There is a sense of order and resigned calm. Men sit outside playing cards or exercising or in the art studio, watching a painting video. Other inmates repair glasses donated by the Lions Clubs that are then sent to those in need all over the world. In other yards prisoners are separated by gang affiliation, history, security level. In the honor yard the inmates mix freely.

On the same unit as the honor yard are buildings A4 and A5, administrative segregation, where Alonza Thomas is being held in solitary confinement five years after his botched attempt to rob the Fastrip food mart. Ten hours a week, Alonza is taken to a small, enclosed yard. The yard can't be seen. There is no dayroom, no interaction. Administrative segregation inmates wear all white. When Alonza leaves the unit, he shuffles in ankle chains, hands cuffed behind his back, a guard on either arm.

Alonza has no radio, no TV. Nothing electric. Alonza has been placed in solitary for his own protection. He snitched on his cell mate, just as years before he snitched on David Foster.[14]

His mother thinks he belongs in a mental hospital. The psychiatrists keep him on medication. Since entering the California

---

14. The prosecutor in that case, Matt Manger, testified on Alonza's behalf on 2000, citing his cooperation in putting a violent felon behind bars.

correctional system, Alonza has been transferred eighteen times, at least seven times for psychological treatment. Sometimes the voices go away. Today the voice he hears is the voice of Samuel Brown, his former cell mate, whose segregated cell is just down the hall. The voice says Alonza is going to be killed.

Nobody gets in to visit administrative segregation. "You would need permission from Sacramento," Ken Lewis says. "And I can tell you right now, they're not going to give it to you." Ken explains the layout of the unit, a design known as a 270, a square with a triangle cut from the center. There are one hundred cells, fifty on top and fifty below, blue doors and small windows. Time like an ocean.

Ken has never heard of Alonza Thomas, but when the case is explained to him, he thinks Alonza could end up in an enhanced psychiatric unit or even a protective custody unit. But it's hard to say. "It's hard to get to a protective custody unit. You have to be Michael Jackson."

The prison in Lancaster is one of fifteen new prisons constructed in the past twenty years to keep pace with the exponential growth of the California inmate population. Designed for 2,200 inmates but housing 4,700, the prison is operating at more than twice its capacity just twelve years after opening. There are 809 peace officers and 442 support services staff, and there is an annual operating budget of $92 million.

Because of the space crunch, medium-security prisoners are kept in dorm beds in the dayrooms of the maximum-security B and C units. The gymnasium houses another 120 beds in forty three-tier bunks. Nobody wants to be on the middle bunk. There is no room for anything except the beds. There is no privacy. The gym inmates are held in the mattress jungle up to twenty hours a day. The medium-security prisoners will all be released someday so are not considered as great an escape threat.

Most maximum-security prisoners are in for life. Because of the overcrowding and the need to separate level III and level IV inmates, each group in B and C is given only two hours in the yard. D unit, the most dangerous—where Alonza was before being sent to isolation—is on lockdown following an inmate riot between the Hispanic and white prisoners earlier in the week.

Ken was a marine and doesn't see a problem with bunking inmates. "Serving the country, I lived in a dorm all the time." He's not unsympathetic, just matter-of-fact. The California prison system already operates on a $7 billion budget. He doesn't think taxpayers should have to pay any more. Some people think prisoners should be given lighter sentences to ease the crowding, but Ken is concerned about the victims. He doesn't think victims would appreciate the idea of releasing criminals because of overcrowding. He's been to victims' group meetings before, and that's what he tells people when they start talking about prison reform. "Go to a victims' group. It will change you. Until you experience that kind of loss, you can never understand."

Ken is a large man with a straight back, a bald head, broad shoulders, and a kind smile. He has worked in prisons most of his life. Prisoners see Ken as an advocate and hope to catch his attention, calling to him from behind the fence. Ken always stops to listen. In five years he'll retire.

"What's with the new shirt?" a guard calls to Ken. "What do you think this is, *Miami Vice*?" Ken says the other day he was wearing a peach shirt, and they didn't like that either. "That wasn't peach," the guard calls back. "It was pink."

Near one o'clock, the hottest part of the day, Ken leaves the prison for the office building on the other side of the perimeter, the iron door closing behind him. There are two hundred prisoners on this side of the fence, in the minimum-security facility. The MSF is for people sent to prison for a couple of months, those caught with small amounts of drugs, or repeat driving-under-the-influence offenders. Lucky for these DUI offenders, no one was killed.

Outside the prison, the wind is slow and warm across the Mojave. In the distance are turbines and the wrinkled foothills of the San Gabriel Mountains. It's an hour and ten minutes to Hollywood. There is a sign for a future veterans' home on a large lot on I Street, and a facility for illegal immigrants being prepared for deportation. The land here is cheap, handsome, and far from view. The landscape is filled with dark squares, nearly all of them being prepped for development. It won't be long before Highway 14 becomes another choked thoroughfare and the last of the county is consumed by the city and its endless network of linked suburbs.

5

While visiting Alonza, Janice witnesses a drug arrest in the visiting area of Lancaster. Something in the force of the action snaps her, and Janice experiences her first panic attack. "Are you OK?" Alonza asks his mother.

She tells her son she can't come by herself anymore. She visits twice more with her youngest son, Patrick, then doesn't visit for four months, despite living only ninety minutes from the facility. At the end of June, she receives a letter from an inmate explaining that Alonza has asked him to write to her if there is an emergency. *You need to check on your son*, he says. *Something bad happen to him.*

When Janice tries to see Alonza, she learns he is in a solitary cell in administrative segregation. Time has to be reserved to meet with the inmate in a special glass-separated enclosure. Appointments must be made on the Friday before the visit. The first time she calls too late. The second and third times she is unable to get through. She leaves messages. Janice receives a note from Alonza, the last prior to the writing of this article:

Dear Mom,

This is your son Alonza hoping and praying that you're in the best of health even though I am not. I am in the hole because I was raped by my celly and they're doing an investigation. I need you to come and see me so I can give you details on what's going to happen to me.

I just want you to realize how scared, confused, and frightened I am. First off I don't know whether or not he had any diseases. And since I told on him I'm considered a snitch and any of his gang friends that see me has to kill me so I'll be forced to go to protective custody or die. Today is Friday. I hope that you come to see me tomorrow so I can tell you how it went down in person.

He's back here too. I can hear him talk to his friends, calling me a snitch. Saying he's going to kill me if he ever sees me, or one of his homeboys from East Coast Crips will kill me. It's driving me crazy. My mental state of mind is shattered. I just don't know what to do. But one thing I do know is that you'll come through as always. I just want to hug you and hear you say that everything is going to be OK. Even though I know it is not.

No matter what happens to me just know that I love my family more than anything. I also pray to Jesus to save me and to get me through this and he talks back. He says this is what has to happen sometimes to get

people to believe that God is real. He tells me he loves
me and that he's here for me through thick and thin.

Alonza

—Los Angeles, 2005

On October 11, 2013, Alonza was released from prison. He was
twenty-eight years old. Most prisoners don't serve their full sen-
tences, but because of his suicidal behavior and other mental
health problems, Alonza served every day of his time.

The Score

1

Lissette told me she was never very sexual with her husband. "In fact, when we were first together, we only had sex maybe twice a day."

I'll let the absurdity of the statement stand for itself. You just have to remember how fragile she is. I have to always remember it, and how fragile I am. We met in a café in Berkeley fifteen months ago, when she was still married. She was reading a fantasy novel, and I wasn't reading anything. We loved each other with one foot out the door. We broke up four times. Or we loved passionately, recklessly. We loved like we didn't care if we lived or died or what the world looked like a week from tomorrow. And then we woke up bored, looked around for who else might be in the room. And she whispered softly in my ear, "We're doomed. It will never work."

2

This is not an essay about breaking up with my girlfriend. I was leaning against the wall of a closed restaurant when I started to write this. Lissette wasn't even home yet; she was still out in the desert, celebrating at the Burning Man festival. I was reading a book about Theo van Gogh, the filmmaker killed by an Islamic fundamentalist in Amsterdam. I had quit taking speed for the most part, but only because it didn't work anymore. I couldn't focus and I was running out of money and I kept making plans and then giving up. I checked out war zones and interviewed celebrities and politicians, but none of it mattered.

Around this time I was in New York, and I got in bed with a twenty-three-year-old volunteer with long, thick red hair. I thought she was Russian, but she said she was Spanish. She was just very pale. I couldn't figure out what to do with her breasts. We were in bed, half-naked, and it was, like, this dead end. It was 2006, two months before the midterm elections. I could have gone for the belt on her jeans, but I had no intention of doing that. I had wanted her, but I had no idea what I wanted from her. I kept asking myself what all of it meant, but you can't ask yourself a question like that and expect any kind of answer.

Around this time I saw a woman walking down Valencia Street in San Francisco wearing a purple nightdress. She was limping, holding the hand of some punk rocker, staggering past the coffee shop. She was almost glamorous, except I was in the Mission, and in the Mission nobody is glamorous except the kids in the street gangs, with their smooth brown skin and blue scarves hanging out of their back pockets.

Around this time I went to dinner with a woman, a sex worker, someone I used to date, someone I dated briefly. I always date briefly, and I always date sex workers because they're the only ones who understand desire without sex. Real desire. Raw and unattainable and without purpose. Desire that ends there, all-consuming, for nothing. We ended up at the back of a restaurant called Delfina, and I told her I was having money problems and couldn't afford a fancy dinner.

She said, "Don't worry."

This particular woman had been raped by her father, and one day a client came to her. The client looked just like her father. She tied the client to a wooden cross, screwed clamps onto his nipples, and beat him until his back was bleeding. The man begged to see her again, but she refused. Or something like that. I told her I have dreams about my father in which I'm holding his ears and scream-ing in his face. My father's old and crippled now. I haven't spoken to him in years.

I held her hand under the table. She had hard palms, strong fingers. She had one more client, so I walked her back, and we lay on her couch for a couple of minutes.

I was just back from Connecticut, where a bunch of true believ-ers were working eighteen hours a day to elect a businessman worth $300 million to the Senate. They were against the war, and he was against the war. I thought, This man has hired and fired people. That's not a statement about character so much as a basic truth. Win or lose, they would all be disillusioned, particularly if he won. They would go home crying.

This was at least half my problem. I was jealous of these people. Their youthful idealism. Even the ones who were older than me. I've worked for politicians. I've been a believer. They've never failed to make a fool out of me and break my heart.

And that's what I was thinking about, the intersection of the half-naked girl, the sex worker with the dark past, and the new politics. But the only place these things met was at me, and I was sitting against what used to be a Kentucky Fried Chicken, trying to figure out what to do with my life. I was tired of hav-ing breakdowns, bored with perpetually standing at the edge of a panic attack. I was going to have to do something, but I wasn't sure what.

3

When Burning Man was over, Lissette called me from Reno. Not immediately; a couple of days later.

She said she didn't want to come home. She was having such a good time. She had that desert voice. The *I don't care about you* voice. It was like a challenge. "I had such a good time," she said. She said she met a guy who was going to teach her how to weld and blow glass. She said she met a guy who was coming to San Francisco to work in the prison, and she told him he could live with her for a couple of months in her studio in the Tenderloin.

She told me all this from inside a hotel room, where she was staying with one of her clients. A client had driven her out to the desert, and another client was driving her home. Lissette worked as a dominatrix. In San Francisco they paid $300 an hour for attention, plus tip. On the open roads of Nevada, littered with the occasional casino, they had her all to themselves for the price of gas. They were happy for her time, but I was less excited. I felt pushed away by her idealized version of herself. This insistence on being happy, even if it was true. She had made promises to herself out on the playa. Promises that included making more art, spending more time with her son, and worrying less about what I thought. She promised herself she would be happy, forgiving, and carefree. Then she danced in front of the fire.

When I saw her, she wore a T-shirt she had just bought at Target and black underwear and sat at her desk with one leg tucked beneath her. Her windows were frosted and closed, but from the top of them I could see some of the buildings in Union Square.

"I wish I had been at Burning Man with you," I said, and she called me a liar.

We talked about her happiness. How she had never been happy with me since we got back together. How we never did anything together. I asked her if she'd fucked anybody in the desert, and she said no. She'd had a platonic boyfriend out there, and at one point they'd sat near the end of the playa, where the mountain rises suddenly, and talked about what might have been.

I thought of how New Orleans had flooded during Burning Man and people had been dancing in the desert while Jefferson

Parish was guarding its bridges with shotguns and people were dying in the New Orleans convention center.

Lissette said she decided to break up with me while she was in the desert. She was staying in a tent village when she made her decision. To make sure she didn't go back on it, she fucked three men and then took two hits of ecstasy and acid. This was different from what she had told me earlier, but I guess she was waiting for her moment.

We were lying in her bed. "I'm waiting for you to talk me out of it," she said.

"How would I do that?" I asked.

"I take it back. I don't want to break up with you. I love you."

"Do you take back fucking those other guys?" I asked. Her leg was over my leg, and she'd pulled my shirt off. I kept grabbing her ass, squeezing. She has the greatest ass I've ever seen. Even when I thought about her fucking other men, all I saw was her ass jiggling up and down and how good that looked.

"Just give me a month," she said, and I asked her why she thought that would work, and she said she needed people to suffer for her and if I would do this, then she would know I was suffering, and then she would love me and I would feel safe and then I wouldn't be distant from her anymore and everything would be fine.

I told her I didn't know. I told her I needed to think about it. I wanted to have sex then. She started playing with my nipple, biting me. I reached between her legs, slid a finger inside her. "Tell me you'll see me again," she said. It was totally unfair, but fair had nothing to do with it. I thought it had to be possible for me to have a real relationship. The kind people have in magazines, that "fulfill" and "facilitate." This had to be open to me, though I'd never experienced anything like it.

I almost said yes, but I didn't. I said, "I don't really care who you fucked out in the desert. The desert is the desert. I know about the music, the lights, and the pills. I'm glad you had a good time. It was probably the greatest display of disposable art ever assembled. Fuck whoever you want." But then I thought, I am in bed with a crazy person and she has tried to hurt me and she will try again. She was aiming an elephant gun at my heart. So I said, "Give me a day to think about it," and that's how she knew it was over.

"You're breaking up with me," she said.

"That's ridiculous," I said.

When I left her apartment, the Tenderloin was full of fog. It floated near my kneecaps. The air was cool and wet, and it wasn't totally dark. There were drug dealers and college students in front of the red-and-green flag of the taqueria. Forty thousand people had gone to the desert carrying art to burn, and pills. A spontaneous, impermanent city.

She would call and say it was over. She would send me a note detailing all the time we'd been together and how she had felt alone. Sitting on a bar stool later that night, I felt the floor shift beneath me. I felt profoundly fucked-up and sad that I hadn't spent the night with her. I wanted to tell my friends about it. I would build up to the punch line: And then she fucked three guys just to make sure she didn't go back on it. And then, get this, she tried to go back on it anyway!

Would I tell them that? Would I mention that she had actually told the men why she was fucking them, and they had fucked her anyway?

4

I think everybody has an Andy Warhol story. I grew up in Chicago. When I think about Andy Warhol, I think about the Kelly house on Sacramento Street. The father was dead, and the oldest of three children had moved out. The younger son was trying to destroy himself, and the daughter was wrecked by the loss of her father.

The place was filled with junkies and house thieves, people I had known all my life. It was like a contained plague. There was shit coming up over the rim of the toilet. There was also this vicious dog that had to be kept locked in the daughter's room upstairs. People were sleeping everywhere, and some of the people were very beautiful. Particularly Justin, who slept with everybody, boys, girls.

There was also Maria, Justin's girlfriend and my first love, who was beautiful and tragic. Her grandmother had kept her locked in the closet and sent her door to door, begging for heroin money, when she was only ten or eleven years old. She used to call me crying, saying she had been masturbating with the vacuum cleaner and she couldn't stop and her thighs were all bruised. Or she would tell me she had walked down to the gas station at night in her underwear and heels. I loved her, but I didn't know what to do about it. We had met in the group homes when we were just fourteen. We had tried for years to find some meeting point where we could comfort each other, but we both wanted basically the same things, and what we needed was someone who wanted something different.

When everything was really going down at the Kelly house, I had already left for college, 150 miles south of the city. But I couldn't stay away. I went up every weekend. I wasn't even getting high then. I spent six years clean and sober; I just didn't want to be alone. And that's what the Kelly house was really about. It was about not being alone. The filth and the drugs were secondary.

It was just like Warhol's Factory in New York, except it was on the North Side of Chicago, the drugs were cheaper, and nobody was ever going to be famous.

I met Ted from the old neighborhood. He was just walking down the street. Turns out we live in the same neighborhood, on the edge of San Francisco. I'm pushing thirty-five now, and he's pushing forty. He asked what I was up to, and I almost started crying. I didn't have a good answer. Of course I was up to things—I was writing *this* essay, for example. I was also working on a screenplay and an oral history of myself. So that's what I told him. But I got kind of choked because it also wasn't true. I wasn't doing anything. The true answer would have been something like, I'm drowning. Or, if I were feeling optimistic, I might have said, I'm recovering. Same thing, really. He asked if I would be getting on the campaign. There were all these races coming up, elections to be held. I said no, not this year. What else could I say about it? I didn't want to leave the city. I didn't want to see another town, another strip mall, another campaign office. I didn't want to be anywhere I was unfamiliar with the public transportation. In fact, I didn't want to go anywhere that wasn't directly on the route between where I lived and where I worked.

I first met Ted at least fourteen years ago, when he was bartending in the Heartland Café and I was just out of college, starting to shoot heroin and strip in the gay bars. Back then he was directing plays at this small storefront theater. He was older than me, not part of my social group, and seemed to have his shit together. He was basically slumming. He came from a good family. His father was an airline executive and owned a penthouse in New York with an atrium. He had been to New York University for dramatic writing. A friend of the family had made a phone call to get him in. One time he slept with my friend Angel's girlfriend, and when Angel asked him why he did it, Ted responded that he did it because he was a writer, and Angel punched him in the face.

Now he's the literary director at a large theater in San Francisco, but we never see each other. I've been in San Francisco eight years already, and we've seen each other maybe five times. His wife, he said, was at home working on a children's book. They owned their own house and had a dog.

He told me they were really happy, and I didn't doubt it. We didn't talk for long. I was on the way to get some nails; I wanted to hang a painting. My ex-girlfriend's slave had made it for me as a housewarming present. I had just moved into a cheaper apartment in a neighborhood where there were a lot of dogs and children, and I was trying to make it livable. I kept thinking, It's OK, I'm not that far away from things.

<h1 style="text-align:center">5</h1>

After the Kelly house had come and gone, when I was just out of college, the world revolved around Michael Jordan and the Chicago Bulls. There were no politics. Bill Clinton was president, and all I knew about him was that he was against welfare and he was putting a lot of people in jail. I would meet my friend Angel at the Beachwood, and we would watch the games on the small TV there with Lisa the social worker and Pat the mailman. The bar owner lived in two rooms attached to the bar.

It was the 1990s. It was Wicker Park. The junkies still shot on Milwaukee Avenue, but the neighborhood was changing. Occasionally Angel and I did heroin or stayed up all night snorting coke at Lisa's apartment down the street, where she lived with her twelve cats and her broken mirrors. But what was really important was the Chicago Bulls.

They could do anything, and if things were really bad, MJ would launch six three-pointers and score thirty-five points in the half. One season we won seventy-two games. They played incredible defense. They would swarm you, knock you off balance, smack the ball away. Scottie Pippen, with those long arms and that crossover dribble. BJ Armstrong, with his boyish good looks. He actually got voted onto the All-Star team just because he had the fortune of passing the ball to Michael Jordan. There was Coach Phil Jackson and Tex Winter, with his fabled triangle offense.

Then Dennis Rodman came along, pulling down fifteen rebounds a game and covered in tattoos. They had to take Dennis's image off the facade of a building because it was causing traffic jams on I-94. I would see Dennis on Sunday nights, when Liquid Soul played at the Double Door. He would lean against the wall near the stage. He was crazy. His birthday party was invitation-only at the Crobar. He fucked Madonna and married Carmen Electra during a Las Vegas bender. He was once caught sitting in a truck in the stadium parking lot with a loaded shotgun under the seat.

In the mid-nineties, everything clicked. We beat Detroit and Portland and Phoenix and Utah and Orlando and New York and Houston. There were all these great players who were never going to wear the rings: Charles Barkley, Karl Malone, Patrick Ewing, and Clyde the Glide. There were all these teams that were good enough to win the championship, but we wouldn't let them. We won every year except when MJ left basketball to play minor-league baseball, and even that year we did good. We built a new stadium on the South Side, with a statue of Michael in front. It was called the United Center, but there was a petition to name it after Jordan's father, who had been killed in a carjacking in South Carolina.

Then I left Chicago for Los Angeles, and basketball didn't matter in the same way. Even though the Lakers now had Shaquille O'Neal, in the bars they left the music on. You could watch the game, but you couldn't *hear* it. People sat at tables, talking over the music, explaining the screenplay they were writing or the film they were producing or the pilot they were acting in. There's a lot of room in Los Angeles. The bars weren't crowded enough. And then I stopped caring.

Later I would decide that politics was the only game for adults, only to realize it wasn't any different from a schoolyard, just a bunch of hurtful insults, character destruction, power grabbing, and coalition building. Meaningless but with consequences. The worst of human nature on display under glass. But early in the new millennium I would follow it just like I had followed basketball. Reading charts, comparing scores, discerning who was on the rise and decline, remembering the stats and rooting crazily, passionately, for my team.

It's only recently, when I'm reevaluating everything, that I realize somewhere in there I made a bad trade. Now I sometimes watch sports with friends, but I get bored. They all have fantasy teams, and they're mostly interested only in how their own players do. I used to read the statistics in the newspapers, but now it's just guys in uniforms on a TV set. Most of the uniforms have a Nike Swoosh.

I'm jealous of my friends who follow sports. They read about football, while I read about the war in Iraq. Of course they read about the war as well, but they don't follow events the way I do. But I'm tired of the war in Iraq and the more shadowy war on terror. The propaganda and he-said, she-said of the daily news cycle. I want to watch the athletes, the very essence of human ambition, gladiators in the stadium, the bright-green turf or the smooth wooden slats. I want to see their long bronze arms extending, fingers reaching from somewhere inside that great huddle of men, all of them leaping in the air, grasping heroically for the ball. And I want to care about the score.

6

I have more to say about my time in Los Angeles. Hollywood is an awful place, and I wasn't even in Hollywood; I was in the Granada Hills, just off the Ronald Reagan Freeway. One day we had a bachelor party. There were strippers there with an Indian bodyguard, and an actor from *Seinfeld*. One of the strippers was drunk, and she grabbed my hair and pulled my head back between her breasts and asked me to tell her she was beautiful. I told her she was and that possibly I was in love with her.

Later the actor was doing shots off the woman's chest. I remember wondering what he was so happy about. He was big and handsome and full of life, and we were in this crappy house in the San Fernando Valley, where everything was just awful dirt and smog. I was staying there, sleeping on a mattress on the floor and jerking off to a forced-feminization magazine someone had left in the bathroom. The magazine was filled with cartoons and stories of men being kidnapped by their girlfriends and fed hormone pills. There were dogs, and I was always stepping in puddles of urine. The actor rented a house in the Hollywood Hills, so things were nicer for him, but I still couldn't get it. He had just landed a part in the next Batman movie. I wished I could be happy like that.

At some point the bridegroom got upset, and then there was violence, the Indian rushing the strippers out the door, the rest of us hanging on to the groom by his limbs. What did anybody expect from us? Violence was all we knew. That guy from *Seinfeld* never came around again. Everybody else left Los Angeles or got into porn. The ones who stayed pushed barbells in strip malls and worked on their cars in front of pale ranch houses, and their lawns filled with so many tools and parts, soon you couldn't see the grass. They folded into the smog and the landscape and disappeared.

Watching the news the other night, I thought about Granada Hills. A reporter had done an exposé on a real estate developer, and he was back to do a follow-up. First the wife came and threw water at the camera. Then the developer arrived. He went right to the reporter and hit him in the face. He pulled back as far as he could and let go with this enormous swing. The reporter had his arms crossed and didn't even try to block it. He was obviously a coward. They fell to the ground, and the cameraman just kept filming. When it was over, the reporter's face was swollen and covered in blood, and the police were taking the real estate developer and his wife away in handcuffs. That's what it's like in Granada Hills, even though this happened in San Diego. Maybe it's the same, all those low houses and so much sun.

7

In better times Lissette used to cut me. She would slice elaborate patterns into my shoulders and stick me with needles. My breathing would slow down when the pins went through me. It was like being on a raft. Everything would be OK. When we were first together, she dug her keys into my back and carved a series of Ls in my skin. The letters were deep and the cuts were ragged and for a while it didn't seem like they would heal, but they did.

I still have scars from my girlfriend before Lissette, who left three marks on my side with a scalpel. Before that I just had marks from a woman in Michigan who burned me with a cigarette on the backs of my hands. Lissette decided to make an E out of the scars on my side, the first of ten letters. She kept a knife by my bed, a present from a client. It had a grip handle. She would tie me up and hold the blade against my throat. One time I was blindfolded and my chest was bleeding and I tried to kiss her, pushing up against the knife, which she held to my jugular.

"You have no sense of self-preservation," she said.

It wasn't true. I had a fantastic sense of self-preservation, but it had left me for a while. I wasn't sure if it would come back.

Lissette used the knife to carve "possession" in my side, but she spelled it wrong. She used only three *s*'s. When I told her, I asked her not to be mad. "It's ruined," she said. Then we broke up. Then we got back together. She recut me, tried to fix it.

It was such an obvious metaphor for our relationship, I didn't even want to think about it. It was like Jim Morrison dying in the bathtub or Ronald Reagan's tax cuts. It meant exactly what you thought it meant.

Between the cutting and the beating and the sex, I could barely move. We would lie in bed for days, until the sheets were covered in blood and lube. She would go home to her husband, but she would be back before I ever recovered. I would try to keep her entertained so she wouldn't leave without giving me my next fix.

I thought of my friend who broke his leg playing football when we were younger, and he was sitting on his bed in the hospital when they came in and wheeled him into the psych ward. His mother had him committed. I used to visit him. They had him in Northwestern, a nice hospital on the lake, much nicer than the place they put me when I was found with my wrist slashed, sleeping in a hallway—a public hospital with shit smeared on the walls. That's what it was like with Lissette. Like being locked in a room. I almost never went out. I missed my friends. I felt like there was nothing I could do.

This is all I know about love.

After Lissette and I broke up, I had to come to terms with my depression. For two years, ever since George Bush was reelected, I had been waiting for the right time to kill myself. The first time in my life I was really suicidal was when I was thirteen. My mother had just died, and I was living on the streets and slashed my wrists. Then I did it again. I made about seven suicide attempts that year before I was locked up.

Things got better after that. The state took custody. There was the mental hospital, then the group homes. I was completely divorced from culture in those days. In the group home we would watch Eddie Murphy movies and listen to house mixes, which didn't interest me at all. I didn't watch television. I read *Catcher in the Rye* and thought it was the worst thing. Who cared about Holden Caulfield? Who cared about rich people who stay in boarding schools and don't know what to do with their lives? That wasn't my environment.

Of course, culture affected me more than I knew. Those house mixes would change music forever. There was a war on drugs going on, and marijuana was getting more expensive. While Joan Didion was in El Salvador, crack was moving into the inner city with the help of the CIA and the administration's ties to the Nicaraguan Contras. It just appeared one day. Hard candy. Cocaine was out of our range, but crack was the drug of the people. We would smoke the rocks in pipes made from pressure gauges and burn our lips.

This was the time of Harold Washington, the first black mayor of Chicago, and all sorts of construction was going on on the South Side, where I lived. There were ribbons in front of buildings and blue-and-white signs with the mayor's name. Washington actually lived in the same neighborhood as the group home, just closer to the lake. When he was reelected, a staff member who dealt drugs on the side took seven of us over there in the house van, and we watched the mayor come out of his building and make a speech.

This wasn't what concerned me. I didn't care about the mayor. Farrakhan was making his move at this time, coming down on the Jews, and his mosque was nearby. So were Jesse Jackson and the Rainbow Coalition. I was beat up in the Garfield train station by people wearing Adidas suits. They stole my gym shoes—Nikes—and I walked home in socks. It all came back to me in the waves of violence and social change that occur in the lowest strata of society, beneath the antenna of mainstream media coverage. We were as important as sand at the bottom of the ocean. We didn't understand that it was the paths of the planets that control the tides. We were too far down to see anything but a thick, dark sky.

8

I sent a letter to my friend Heathen. I said, *Gosh, you know.* I said I wanted to be somewhere safe but public. I wanted to be on a leash or have a bit in my mouth. I didn't want to be expected to speak. I had been in the papers recently for a book I'd written. My father had responded by sending letters to the editors insisting there was nothing wrong with me. I hadn't been abused; I was just spoiled. He complained to one reporter, "He's not damaged. My son is a success." He told anyone who would listen that those group homes were actually very nice places.

I told Heathen I was just finishing an essay that would combine everything I'd ever seen and end with a man standing in front of a chasm, preparing to jump. But I didn't want to jump. I wanted to be naked and available and wanted. I didn't want to know who was doing what. I didn't want to engage with the politicians, the missing ballots in Prince George's County. I thought about Daniel Pearl saying, "I am a Jew. My mother is a Jew." I thought about Theo van Gogh, Mohammed Bouyeri stepping from the shadow. Theo begging for mercy. "Don't do it. Don't do it." First a bullet, then several more. Then Bouyeri slits his throat, pins his manifesto to Theo's chest with a dagger, and Amsterdam is never the same again.

I lived in Amsterdam. It was 1992, and I was a barker for a live sex show called the Casa Rosso. I was dating a hooker from Australia and then Miriam, a Surinamese cabaret dancer whose husband was in jail for murder. It was the first time a woman ever took me home, tied me up, and slapped me without my paying for it. I didn't know anything about the world in 1992. It would be thirteen years before I fell in love.

In my letter I told Heathen I wanted to be penetrated and pierced and laughed at and pulled along by my hair. I wanted to be objectified. I wanted to be restrained and suffocated. I wanted to be slapped and talked down to. I had just come back from Israel, seen the smoke rising from the Lebanese villages beyond the hills, stared into the muzzle of a tank, witnessed the jet hovering still in the sky while Caterpillar D9s churned the soft red soil along the border. I walked along the fence watching for snipers, clenching my fists and pressing them against my head. I spoke with residents in deserted towns terrified to walk down the street. Realized for the first time that war is not about destruction, it's about fear.

I told Heathen I'd lost my girlfriend to the new sexual politics. I said I wanted a strap-on forced in my mouth while the girl wearing the strap-on spoke with her friends. I wanted pictures to be taken and posted everywhere. I didn't want to have sex, but I wanted to be penetrated. I didn't want to go down on anybody, but I wanted to be sat on by people wearing clothes. I wanted to be the only one naked.

There was a war going on between cultures. There was a new crusade, but the weapons were bigger. I apologized for being selfish. It had nothing and everything to do with the controversial Dutch filmmaker. The great conflict of the new century had moved into direct and violent contact with the outer limits of the Enlightenment. One man—deranged, on the edge of society, an immigrant's son, discriminated against, lacking opportunities, caught in the worldwide web of militant Islam. The Internet jihadist porn store, filled with dirty videos of beheadings, throat slittings, a boot pressing into a woman's stomach while a geyser of blood erupts from her neck, martyr glorification, bearded men holding guns and smiling for the camera before leaving to seek their death. All of these found on a short stack of DVDs in Bouyeri's apartment. And the other man, the one he killed, a minor celebrity, an attention seeker, a Dutch Bill O'Reilly. A man full of hate and convenient ideologies, a nationalist, a xenophobe, a grandnephew of one of the greatest painters the world has ever known.

A woman screamed at Bouyeri as he reloaded his gun, "You can't do this!"

"Yes, I can," he replied.

It was two years after Theo van Gogh's ugly murder. My girlfriend was fucking three men in a tent, in a city that had sprung up in a week, with forty thousand naked wanderers, all of them covered in a thin film of white dust, looking to get high. A dry mecca of disposable art. They would burn everything.

"That's when I decided to leave you," she said. I don't think she had ever heard of Theo van Gogh, though I'm sure she'd visited the Van Gogh Museum as well as the Anne Frank House.

Later, Lissette would leave a brief note and a small pile of my possessions on my doorstep. Inside these things, in a white box, would be a clear plastic bag, and inside that a sugarcube full of acid and a capsule full of ecstasy. She hoped I would see what she saw. The pills and the sugar would help me understand. Like Rex Hofman, who drinks a cup of coffee in order to find out what happened to his wife, who disappeared three years earlier, and he wakes up in a coffin, buried alive.

Later, I would send a note to Heathen explaining everything I wanted in the current political climate. I told her I wanted what everybody else wants; it's just the details that are different. I see connections everywhere I look. It's not that it doesn't make sense; it makes perfect sense, it's just that lives are fractured. I can easily keep this many balls in the air. This is who I am. This is the world right now.

I finished the note by saying I wanted to be afraid and I wanted to cry with someone who's not afraid to make me sad, who doesn't stop just because I'm crying.

Heathen wrote me back. She said she wanted the same thing.

—San Francisco, 2007

The Business
of America
Is Business

What was everyone doing? Everyone was getting by.

Why Britney Matters

It's Britney, bitch. That's the opening to the first single released from *Blackout*, Britney Spears's sex-and-drugs masterpiece.

I'm not sure what led me to the point in life where I'm listening to Britney Spears on repeat. It started while I was writing about a murder trial, a trial that I almost got thrown out of—the judge calling me to chambers, three lawyers and two cops sitting around his desk. He wanted to know if I had been talking to a juror. I had seen the juror at the train and said hello. The juror wrote a three-page memo detailing our conversation, which the judge waved in front of me. He was deciding whether or not to bar me from the court. All I could say was "I'm sorry." I returned to my pew, passing the smiling accused murderer, seated at the end of a long table in the middle of the court. It was a sympathetic smile, his bright-red lips twisted to points on his cheeks, like the smile of Jack Nicholson's Joker. He was commiserating with me, trying to say: It sure is hard to stay out of trouble around here!

But that doesn't really explain Britney or her new album, *Blackout*. That's just where I was in my life, immersed in crime, making bad decisions, scattered. Like the rest of America, I saw Britney's disaster on MTV, lazying around a stripper pole like a cat on Valium. That was enough for me. I downloaded the rest of the album, and then her earlier albums, and I started trying to understand what I had been missing, what the teenage girls always knew.

Every day I woke before six a.m. to spend three to four hours trying to place what I'd seen into a coherent narrative before heading to court. I needed music that wouldn't challenge me in any way. I sat at the table in my small room, staring at an air shaft, the sound of my roommate shifting noisily on the other side of our thin wall replaced with earbuds piping Britney Spears, who was twenty-six years old and the seventh-best-selling female artist of all time.

It's challenging to engage in a serious conversation about Britney Spears. My friends are proud of their musical taste, and I frequently embarrass them, but there are limits. Over time, derivative acts such as Stone Temple Pilots and Everclear have gained a grudging hipster acceptance. Ten years from now, I predict, we'll think about Nickelback in an entirely different way.[1] Despite selling 80 million albums, it's doubtful Britney will ever be appraised as anything more than a signifier of other, more relevant cultural trends. The intelligentsia doesn't even consider her a musician. She's barely a vessel. One friend tells me that Britney Spears is a wholly manufactured sound and that the only difference between Britney and a computer program is her ability to walk onstage.

But it's not true. Britney has a way of dipping at the end of a verb like she's having an orgasm so intense and fast, the only thing to do is dance right through it. Other times she's forceful, or innocent; she always feels it at exactly the right time. She doesn't have "pipes" like Mariah or Christina. What she has is a sweet Southern drawl that tells a story, which is strange, because it's a story she doesn't seem to understand. Her songs contradict each other; as she gets older, her schoolgirl drawl is ripping

---

1. I no longer stand by this prediction.

in two, leaving a ragged, adult edge evidenced on almost all the songs on what is her best album by far. It's the sound of a voice at its peak, about to go into steep decline.

Much of the criticism of Britney is based on the fact that she doesn't write her own songs. If she did, it's likely the rest of her transgressions would be easily forgiven. After all, artists are supposed to be self-centered and crazy. I have to remind people that Elvis didn't write his own songs either.

"Are you comparing Britney to Elvis?"

"Yes, I am."

Remember, Elvis wanted to lead the war on drugs. He arranged a meeting with Richard Nixon on this very topic. He showed up to meet the president of the United States stoned out of his mind and wearing a cape. And not just any cape, but a half cape that went to his elbows like an unfinished Batman costume. Tell me Elvis is a genius, I'm not going to disagree with you. But can we agree on what the word "genius" means? The word "genius" almost always begs for a modifier—a musical genius, a physical genius, an empathic genius. Sometimes I wonder if these qualified terms aren't interchangeable with "talented idiot."

I'm talking here about Britney Spears performing at the Super Bowl wearing socks on her hands. Compare that high-energy performance with the totem-faced members of the Rolling Stones, swinging their guitars over their craggy shoulder blades. Apples and oranges, of course. The Stones write their own music and play their own instruments. They were never chosen; they insisted on taking the stage. Without any help from anyone else, the Rolling Stones are still a great band. Britney is just a performer. It's like comparing an actor and a director. Let's get back to that "genius" word for a minute. Stanley Kubrick is indisputably a genius. Tom Cruise, not so much. But I'd still rather hear Tom say, "Worship the cock." And I'd rather watch Spears dancing with socks on the wrong appendages than four old men clapping their hands over their heads. And I love the Rolling Stones. I'm just saying.

Her unquestioning trust in her producers is a hallmark of her sound. Cluelessness pervades her music—a deliberate ignorance of larger societal issues, lyrics shocking in their meanness, all of it layered over a pitch-perfect delivery and simple, unforgettable beats. How many people could remove themselves so entirely from the process until called upon, at which point they slip into their role like a spoon into soup?

Which is to say that Britney Spears is more complex than she's given credit for. Take her debut album, . . . *Baby One More Time*. At first glance, the target audience would seem to be pedophiles. But it's not. There she is in her video, in shiny, flat, round-toed shoes, socks to her knees this time, a short skirt, a jacket open to expose her belly button, dancing in the school hallway. She shakes her chest, then sways her hips in a way that's more of a promise than a suggestion. Her skirt flashes open, baring the tops of her thighs. Inhibited schoolgirls in starched button-ups look approvingly from behind open lockers, like they've been given permission to live, though in real life they're professional dancers, some with coke habits. What's going on here? Britney is wearing pigtails with pink ribbons, and a quarter inch of lipstick, singing, *My loneliness is killing me*. Not likely. But that's not what this is about. The call is to teen girls in sheltered suburban environments preparing to break the chains of their generation's expectations. And they do, for a moment. Then they go back to their schoolwork, then college, then they're married with a kid on the way. Soon they'll be chastising their own children, running out the door of the Montessori school, screaming, "Come back here, little missy! You look like a whore!"

Britney is the opposite of that. Britney doesn't fade into obscurity. Britney goes all the way.

At the end of that video, Britney is back in class. It was all just a dream. Though obviously it wasn't—she's still wearing a full tube of lipstick. In her next album, the pining schoolgirl returns in a red-leather catsuit to tell us that she's not that innocent, that she's a self-satisfied heartbreaker. She doesn't care about other people at all. She has the same inviting smile, but it's no longer friendly. In fact, she might not be capable of love. "Oops! . . . I Did It Again" has more to say about the Britney phenomenon and is perhaps why so many smart people loathe her. It's too much to be expected to empathize with this greedy, beautiful creature. *I played with your heart, got lost in the game.* But hey, she's just the messenger.

Fast-forward past the Pepsi commercial, though it is impressive to note that Britney can sing a ballad about a soda with the same conviction as any of her songs. Her "genius" is transferrable. My father used to tell me a good writer can write about anything and make it interesting, but I've never believed that. An author has to be interested in his subject. Britney doesn't have that problem. Or perhaps she's just passionate about everything.

Fast-forward past *In the Zone*, a worthless album with the exception of "Toxic." Fast-forward past Britney's cover of "I Love Rock 'n' Roll," which should be enough to convince anyone that this no-longer-a-girl, not-yet-a-woman is in possession of a unique and terrifying talent, irrespective of the vacuum it may exist in. Past the marriage to the backup dancer and the two children. Stop on the best track on *Blackout*, "Piece of Me."

Every star at this point in their career puts out a song like this, an angry or wistful ballad about the difficulty of being recognized, misunderstood, and exploited. But Britney's version is one of the best. This song is so infectious, so basic, that when you hear it the first time, it's like you've heard it a hundred times before. In fact, you've already got it memorized. It reminds me of a pornographic novel that held my interest for a couple of years. I read that book at least once a month, despite its lack of literary merit and its having no ending (the author stopped at the half-way point, having painted himself into a corner). I read it more times than anything I've read before or since. "Piece of Me" has everything in common with that unfinished tome. A pornographic novel doesn't need to make sense; pornographic music doesn't either. It just feels good. You don't have to think about it at all, just nod your head and do your work. Or you could listen closer, fall off that ragged edge I was talking about—you might get an idea of where this is going.

Britney is having her perfect moment. If you want a piece, the time is right now. Despite shaving her head, flashing the paparazzi, losing her children to K-Fed, or the other things that have absolutely no relation to her music, when she says, *You want a piece of me*, she's right. The only flaw, the only line in the whole song that accidentally snags on the listener's intellect, is when Britney says,

I'm Mrs. "Most likely to get on the TV for strippin' on the streets"
When getting the groceries, no, for real,
Are you kidding me?
No wonder there's panic in the industry
I mean, please.

When you take that last piece of Britney, the playful horror of grocery shopping, there's nothing to do but let it go—the synthetic slide guitar is intersecting the sounds pouring from her beautiful lips at just that moment. She's been Miss American Dream since she was seventeen. Nine years later, did you really think she was shopping for her own groceries? Do you shop for yours?

—*San Francisco, 2008*

The DIY Book Tour

I arrived early—I'm always early—at a house in Chesterfield, Virginia, a short drive from Richmond, down the Powhite Parkway. This was the fifteenth city I'd been to. I had given a reading the night before at a home in a nearby town, and when I mentioned Chesterfield, people made sour faces. But I go where I'm invited.

The small house was on a street filled with similar houses and well-tended front yards. My host explained that she was a nurse at a hospital in Richmond, and Chesterfield was the closest place she could afford. She had just moved in, and there wasn't much furniture, just twenty white folding chairs not yet arranged.

Nineteen of her friends showed up, and we spread out into the living room and small kitchen. Many of them also worked at the hospital. One was a professional jujitsu fighter and personal trainer, another a real estate agent. None of them had ever been to a literary event before. Several told me they were big readers, at least a book a week. But when I asked about their reading habits, they hadn't heard of the authors who are famous in my world: Lorrie Moore, Roberto Bolaño, Michael Chabon. This is most of America, I thought. I've stepped through the door.

Originally, my publisher had a standard tour planned: five bookstores in five large coastal cities. The early reviews were strong, and one friend, a successful author, encouraged me to do a larger tour. But the idea depressed me. This was my seventh book. I have my following, but I'm not famous. I didn't want to travel thousands of miles to read to ten people, sell four books, then spend the night in a cheap hotel room before flying home. And my publisher didn't have the money for that many hotel rooms, anyway.

I decided to try something I hoped would be less lonely. Before my book came out, I set up a lending library, allowing anyone to receive a free bound galley on the condition that they forward it within a week to the next reader, at their own expense. Four hundred people had participated in the lending library, and I wrote this group and asked if people wanted to hold an event in their homes. They had to promise twenty attendees. I would sleep on their couches. My publisher would pay for some of the airfare, and I would fund the rest by selling the books myself.

When you read in people's homes, you're reading to a reflection of their world. In Lincoln, Nebraska, I read in the home of Ember Schrag, a twenty-five-year-old folk-rock musician. She plastered the town with flyers, but the people who came were all in their twenties and into rock 'n' roll. In Las Vegas I read at Laurenn McCubbin's house. She's a painter, and her primary subjects are adult entertainers. Many people in attendance were either artists or sex workers or both.

The people who attended the readings had usually not heard of me. They came because it was a party at their friend's house and the friend promised to make those cupcakes they like or they were coming as a favor. Nobody wants to give a bad party, and touring this way ensured there would be at least one person other than me who would be embarrassed if no one else arrived.

The readings mostly went long, more than an hour with questions, and people didn't leave. We were often up talking until one in the morning. An important part of the book is my troubled relationship with my father and what I took to be his confession to murder in an unpublished memoir. (I investigated and found no evidence of any such killing; my father refused to confirm or deny it.) Following the reading, over a glass of wine or slice of cake or nothing at all, people told me about their own difficult relationships with family members, people they couldn't forgive or who wouldn't forgive them. The readings felt like an extension of the book.

At a reading in West Seattle, I sat in a corner. The attendees surrounded me on a large sectional sofa with extra seats. The host had stacked my books on the mantelpiece. Nobody asked about my writing process, or how to find an agent or a publisher. Unlike at every reading I've done for every other book I've written, there were no aspiring writers in attendance. One of the guests asked about my mother—why isn't she a bigger part of the story?

The person hosting the reading usually picked me up at the airport or bus station. Then I met their friends and tried to sell them books, like they were Tupperware. Altogether, I sold about 1,100 books (not counting copies of my older books, which I was also selling) at seventy-three events. Seven hundred of those were books I'd purchased wholesale; a few hundred more were sold by local booksellers.

A lecturer invited me to read at her small college in Ohio. I read to undergraduates in the coffee shop in the bottom of the English building. Most of the students looked like they were in high school, but one of them bought a book. She had a firm grip and I asked her how old she was and she said she was just getting used to saying she was eighteen. Another student was waiting, but the last student in line didn't want to buy a book.

"I don't have any money," she said.

"That's OK," I said. "I'll put my address inside and you can send me a check."

She thought about it for a second. "No," she said. She wasn't going to have any money anytime soon. Then she asked about writing from experience. She said she was afraid to expose herself in her own writing.

When I'm writing a book, I feel like I'm in a cave. It's so lonely. I come out of the cave years later, surprised to see the sun.

I've published all my books with small presses. When someone asks me to explain the book tour, I tell them about the time I was traveling in Australia. We hiked to the top of a mountain using topographical maps and then belayed on ropes into the canyon. We dropped deeper until we were in a place that was darker than anywhere I'd ever been. There was a stream running alongside us and an echo of a waterfall in the distance. Then the walls were covered in glowworms. We turned on our headlamps, and the glowworms disappeared. We had been warned of the possibility of flash floods, and if there was a flood, none of us would survive. But there weren't any floods that day, or rain, and we emerged into a forest that seemed so bright, I was certain we would run into Snow White or one of the dwarfs. We'd been hiking for hours and I was in the same shape as my friends and I fell a couple of times, cutting open my chin on a rock. The final hike was different from the trek through the canyon but still a part of the whole.

In other words, the book tour is part of the book.

I did one of the best readings of my life at that reading in Ohio for forty college students and sold fewer than ten books. At fancy homes, I sold more books than there were people in attendance.

Not everything worked out. At a home in Boston, I read to seven people. During the discussion a graduate student who had returned to Harvard to study government announced, "You must be tired of talking about yourself."

Nobody bought a book that night, and on the way out the same woman urged me to "keep writing."

In Chesterfield, after an hour of getting to know one another, we set up the folding chairs, and people sat politely in rows. I read leaning against the kitchen breakfront. They asked interesting questions about murder and confession and the moment when I describe lies mixing with the truth like red and yellow paint becoming orange, the original colors ceasing to exist. Afterward people went back to talking, grabbing another drink or a snack.

—New York, 2010

An Interview with Lorelei Lee

The first sex work I ever did, I was nineteen. It was mostly photos of me stripping and fake masturbating. Then I made this recording pretending that I was talking about the first time that I gave a blow job or something. The guy who did that shoot now owns Naughty America. It's a huge porn company and they have, like, twelve websites. I was nineteen and he was eighteen and just starting. Now he has a million dollars and I don't.

Then I moved to San Francisco. I worked in a coffee shop for two years, quit, and started posing naked for anyone who would hire me.

Kink.com was advertising on this website, offering $400 for a four-hour shoot, more money than I had ever made. I called, and it was Marty, who now runs Sex and Submission and Whipped Ass. I told him I didn't have any pictures because I didn't like the pictures I had. He said to just come down to the studio. I knocked on the door of this unmarked warehouse building. Somebody let me in and introduced me to Marty. I took my clothes off and did a little spin. He took Polaroids and said, "Yeah. We'll call you."

Soon after that I did my first shoot with Peter Acworth for Hogtied. I curled my hair and wore false eyelashes, and I thought I looked ridiculous. I didn't really know how to put on makeup. It was an abduction scene, and he grabbed me on Eighth Street with a cloth over my face and I screamed really loud. People were staring, and he pulled me into the building. When we got inside he said, "Thank God we had the camera. We would have been arrested." Then he tied me up, tore my clothes off, flogged my tits. I don't remember everything. I remember being really excited about it, feeling really in my body in a way I hadn't felt before. I went home afterward. I was exhausted and had bruises all over me. My roommates were a little freaked-out, and they were like, OK, that's what she's doing now.

Two months after that Kink took me to BondCon in Las Vegas. All of a sudden I felt like a movie star. We would hang out at the booth and pose for pictures and these guys would come through and say, "Oh yeah. I saw you on the Internet." I knew I was making these movies, but it didn't occur to me that there was an audience. At BondCon I met Adrianna Nicole. She helped me learn how to dress and wear makeup. I felt we were kind of in it together.

Porn was an incredibly therapeutic thing for me. I got to go into rooms with people and experiment with being vulnerable in a place where I had no emotional responsibility. I went into work and people said, "What do you want to do today? What don't you want to do today?" Nobody had ever asked me that before in terms of sex. I could decide at any time that I never wanted to go back. I had to be there for four hours for the shoot, and I got to deal with whatever the emotions were afterward on my own.

In 2005, I did my first boy-girl scene. I was like, OK, I'm really a whore now. Kink had become a bigger company, working with girls from L.A., hiring through agencies. The girls from L.A. told me how they worked all the time. I only worked every couple of weeks. I felt like maybe it was the next thing. I had done everything at Kink: boy-girl, two boys, location shoots, suspensions, and all the blah, blah, blah. It stopped feeling new to me. I didn't feel like I was accomplishing things. So I decided to go to L.A. And there was money, of course. I couldn't imagine working every day for that much money.

I called Adrianna's agent, Mark Spiegler. I said, "I'll do everything." He said, "Buy a ticket."

He picked me up, and we went to dinner at a deli. I already had shoots lined up for that week. I met Annette Schwartz, who I fell in love with. We lived together at Spiegler's. Everybody said we were girlfriends.

Spiegler is this older man in his fifties, and he is very controlling and I think he would be lonely if he didn't have girls living in his house. He was this father figure. We had curfew, and he drove us everywhere. It was like being a teenager. But he approached it like a businessman. He would encourage us to work all the time. He said it was for our own benefit. If you don't work, people forget who you are. At the time I believed everything he said, but later I started to think everything was for him. He was getting his cut, but I don't think that was it. We had this sort of weird dysfunctional family going on, and I think that was a huge part of it for Spiegler. But I don't think there was anything sinister about him. He's a sweet and lonely guy. He would never try to hit on us or anything like that. He looks the way you think a porn agent is going to look. He's got a big belly, and he's always wearing these T-shirts that have funny sayings. He always said, "I wouldn't mess with the girls. It's bad for business. Then they get jealous of each other. I have to lock my door at night. I'm scared of them."

There was also George, our driver. He was younger, and we would complain to him about Spiegler. I loved George. He was this tough gangster type, and he would show up on set like Mr. Tough Guy. If somebody tried to pay you less . . . I shouldn't name names, but one director in particular had me and Annette on set and we're doing a blow bang and there's four guys and the director wants to be in the scene too, and he's saying, "Well, you guys are basically only doing two blow jobs each because there's two of you and four of them." And I was like, "No fucking way. Obviously we're both giving four blow jobs, and if you're going to be in it, that's going to be five, and you have to pay us for five blow jobs."

I was flying back and forth for a year and a half, spending two to three weeks a month in L.A. I lived out of a suitcase the whole time and felt very disconnected from my friends in San Francisco. I couldn't take a class. I felt alienated from the world, except for porn. I couldn't talk to people in the grocery store. I still feel this way.

I flew back for a week of shoots. There was a new Spiegler girl, and I came in and she said hi and I went in the other room and started crying. Spiegler came in and said, "All right. You don't want to do it. You're going to be crying more when you don't have any money." I said, "I don't know if I can." And he said, "Can you just come in tomorrow?" Then I did the week, and I was fine.

I decided I needed a break. I came home and signed up for a class. At State I felt exposed, because the other thing about working all the time is that I never had to be in a room with a lot of people who weren't in porn. I was kind of depressed. I was scared because I thought I couldn't keep making porn and I couldn't do anything else. I got a job as a waitress and I worked and I went to school. I got a boyfriend. I hadn't dated anyone in years. I had been having all this sex, and I hadn't had any personal sex in a very long time. I was still performing at Kink occasionally. I was starting to feel better about myself, starting to feel sexy again. And then I did the Sex Workers' Art Show. For six weeks I was on tour with all these amazing queer sex workers who felt really good about themselves. I was going to go back to L.A. after the tour, but I didn't. I called in sick the night before I was supposed to go back.

Now I work for Kink once a week, sometimes more. The difference is that I have my whole life.

In the end you do all this stuff, and you're like, That was something, but what? I would look at these pictures of these mainstream porn girls. I thought they looked beautiful. The girl in the picture is always smiling. She's not the girl who's alone in her room. In BDSM you don't get pretty pictures. The Kink shoots were fun, but they weren't glamorous. I had this feeling that I was not good enough, pretty enough. I wanted to be the girl in the picture.

Sometimes I get emails. They tell me I'm beautiful, they tell me I'm a whore, it's all the same. They don't know anything about me. People come up to me in a bar and say, "You look familiar." But they don't know why I look familiar. In real life I'm just a girl. On the Internet, on their computer screen, on their TV screen, I'm the embodiment of their sexual fantasies. But their sexual fantasies are wrapped up in every other part of who they are. I have this one guy who has been writing me for years. He tells me I'm like his little sister. He says he's in love with me and thinks we could have had this amazing relationship if I hadn't ruined it. It's not really threatening. There have been times when I felt sensitive, but for the most part I just think it's fascinating. I think, Look at all these lonely people out there. Why are they writing to me? It's like a window into the insides of all these people. Sometimes I feel a little less fucked-up.

I'm an adult now and I make these choices because I'm doing what's best for me. It's not because I'm programmed by some trauma; it's because I'm doing the best I can to make my life the best it can be.

—*San Francisco, 2009*

Silicon Is Just Sand

1. THE ACCUSED

August 29, 2015, is a hot night on Venice Beach. Normally the superheated inland desert sucks the damp air off the ocean, blanketing the coast with a layer of moisture all the way to the 405. But tonight, something has gone wrong. There's no fog, and the sky is boiling, even at two a.m.

A dark SUV pulls in front of the Cadillac Hotel, a two-star lodging better known for its cheap rooms and stained carpets than its views of the ocean. The car's lights wash over a homeless man sitting on the sidewalk. The homeless live all over Venice Beach and have for as long as anyone can remember, particularly at the northern end of the boardwalk, on the edge of Santa Monica. Their tents line the small, grassy hills between the sidewalk and sand. Stuffed sleeping bags, shopping carts, signs and bedding made from cardboard. You almost wouldn't know how much this place has changed recently.

The SUV's lights stay on, illuminating the scene as Sris Sinnathamby, the owner of the Cadillac Hotel, steps out of the passenger side. He's followed by the driver, identified by multiple witnesses as Francisco Cardenaz Guzman. Guzman is known to the police as a member of the Venice 13, a gang with ties to the Sureños, who control the local drug trade. He has been arrested many times, for gun possession, robberies, and car theft.

Sinnathamby and Guzman have just returned from James'

Beach bar, a five-minute drive down the street. Sinnathamby walks up to a homeless man and tells him to get away from the front of the hotel. A security camera at a nearby café records the scene.

Sinnathamby is not like Guzman. He was born in Sri Lanka and came to the United States in his twenties. He happened to be passing through Venice twenty-five years ago when he ran out of money and took a job cleaning hotel rooms at the Cadillac, then worked his way up to manager. When the owner retired, Sinnathamby bought the place from him. It's not fancy, but it faces the ocean, and, pretty or not, it has dramatically risen in value in the past decade.

The run-up in real estate prices has been driven in part by the explosion of tech companies along the beach on the west side of Los Angeles. Google, Snapchat, Hulu, BuzzFeed, YouTube, Netflix, and Facebook have overtaken an archipelago of properties, bringing an influx of programmers, sales executives, and the refined retail that follows such a massive migration of well-paid people. They call it Silicon Beach.

The homeless don't necessarily mind the newcomers, but the newcomers mind the homeless. Sinnathamby is not one of the newcomers, but they have been very good for his businesses. In addition to the Cadillac, Sinnathamby owns the gourmet eatery Dudley Market, a parking lot on Ocean Front Walk, and other Venice properties. Sinnathamby again tells the homeless guy to get moving. The man rises and shuffles toward the boardwalk, twenty feet away.

In 2012, a law made it illegal to sleep on the boardwalk from midnight to five a.m. The justification was public safety. Homeless advocates have filed lawsuits challenging the ordinance. In the meantime the homeless feel harassed, with people always kicking their feet, telling them to move. Venice is a place with a long history of art and activism, and now, a flood of wealth. Tempers run high on all sides.

.   .   .

Sinnathamby's efforts to move the homeless man attract the attention of a group of nearby boardwalk denizens. "Leave him alone," says Shakespeare, a twenty-six-year-old rapper and poet who frequently sleeps on the boardwalk near the Cadillac. Sinnathamby walks over to him, passing a man pushing a cart, who exchanges greetings with Sinnathamby. Everyone knows one another.

The homeless have been drinking. They had a party earlier on Hippie Hill, a mound of grass nearby, to celebrate Shakespeare completing a new recording. Shakespeare argues with Sinnathamby, insisting the man has a right to stay on the sidewalk. But then Guzman, who has so far hung back on the boardwalk by himself, suddenly pulls out a gun and fires four shots down the beach. Shakespeare gets even more agitated, gesturing toward Guzman as if to challenge him. Sinnathamby stands between the two men, keeping them apart. Guzman waves his gun in a threatening manner.

Two women, friends of Sinnathamby's who were waiting in the SUV, now get out and walk over to him. He turns to the women, and as he does, Shakespeare shifts to his right and lunges at Guzman. Guzman notices Shakespeare and shoots him three times, stepping aside like a bullfighter as Shakespeare falls past him, exiting the frame of the surveillance video. Guzman waits for a moment, then gestures for the women and Sinnathamby to come with him. But they stay. Finally Guzman runs to the SUV and drives away. At least that's how it all appears on the video.

The ocean is as calm as a sheet of paper.

2. THE JOURNALIST

Nine days later, I arrive in Venice. I move into a small two-bedroom with a roommate on Pacific and Breeze, one block from the beach, four blocks from the Cadillac Hotel. It's ferociously hot, and like most places so close to the ocean, this one has no air-conditioning. I have a small carry-on bag with me, a pair of jeans, two T-shirts, a pair of shorts. No return ticket.

On the boardwalk near my apartment, some people and local community organizations have erected a memorial for Shakespeare at the base of one of the boardwalk's pagodas— the usual candles and flowers, a pink bow, a poster signed by his friends, a framed picture of Shakespeare in a tan jacket, a stuffed panda bear. A group of homeless men and women lounge in the pagoda, one of only a handful of slivers of shade.

I've been sent here by a magazine to figure out why Google has moved into so many buildings in the area, why there are so many accelerators and shiny new coworking spaces. Snapchat chose Venice over Silicon Valley and is now valued at $20 billion, with more than eight hundred employees. What is happening here? That's my assignment.

I'm not a tech reporter; I don't have any particular expertise in real estate. I'm forty-three and I've lived a lot of lives. I've been homeless. I've worked for a start-up. I've sabotaged myself and my relationships and been fired many times. I've been ripped off and overpaid in equal measure. I've overdosed, worked in politics, fund-raised, hosted, waited, bused, Kickstarted. I was a dedicated climber until I wasn't. I spent a season snowboarding, living on a mountain. I spent three months in a mental hospital when I was an adolescent and fourteen years later taught undergraduate creative writing at Stanford. I've said "I love you" more times than I've actually been in love.

Venice has lived a lot of lives too. One-hundred and thirty years ago, Venice was conjured into existence by Abbot Kinney, a wealthy tobacco magnate from New Jersey, who in the beginning of the twentieth century won the swampland south of Santa Monica in a coin toss with his business partners. Kinney was determined to build his own version of Venice, Italy, the floating city he fell in love with on one of his many trips abroad.

Kinney brought architects and engineers from Boston; he hired laborers to build miles of trenches and an amusement pier, a lecture hall, and a boardwalk. On June 30, 1905, ocean water began flowing through two enormous pipes at a rate of five hundred gallons a second, filling the canals. Venice of America opened on July 4, 1905. Kinney hired the best lecturers and performers of the time, including Sarah Bernhardt and symphony orchestras. By 1910, Venice had more than 3,000 residents and was drawing 50,000 to 150,000 tourists on weekends.

Kinney died suddenly in 1920. Without him, Venice foundered. Half the canal developments remained unfinished; the piers burned multiple times; the city couldn't maintain its own infrastructure. In 1925, Venice voted to join Los Angeles.

The city paved over most of the canals in anticipation of the great automobile influx. Then, like a neglectful parent, Los Angeles turned its back on Venice. By the 1950s, the area had become known as the Slum by the Sea. In the late fifties, drawn by the cheap rents and the ocean breeze, the artists started arriving. Dennis Hopper opened a studio, along with Ed Ruscha. There was an explosion of poetry and art as the beat generation settled in. The beats were joined by the flower children. Venice was brimming with bohemian creativity. Janis Joplin showed up in 1960. Jim Morrison lived in the sidewalk villages, partying and writing poetry on various rooftops near the ocean. When Morrison met Ray Manzarek on Venice Beach, he told Manzarek, "I was taking notes at a fantastic rock-and-roll concert going on in my head."

But the hippies and the artists weren't the only outsiders flocking to Venice. It's also where Arnold Schwarzenegger and Franco Columbu came to get huge, at Muscle Beach. And it's where the

Z-Boys took skateboarding mainstream in the abandoned Pacific Ocean Park. It's where Suicidal Tendencies combined punk rock and heavy metal and where Jane's Addiction created the bridge between metal and grunge bands like Nirvana.

Venice is like that kid who overcommits to everything. She comes to college, joins the cheerleading squad, dates the quarterback. By her senior year she has tattooed her face, gotten eighteen piercings, and occupied the administration building. A few years later she's living in a commune, eating only raw food. Then maybe she finds religion or joins a cult or has a child. You could argue she's never had anything but religion. She's a believer, and when she believes in something, she believes in it all the way.

Which might be part of what I relate to about this place. I've always lived my life like I'm about to jump out the second-story window of a burning house.

3. THE LANDLORD

I spend a week mostly swimming in the ocean and eating pizza on the boardwalk, surrounded by souvenir shirts presenting dreadlocked skeletons smoking joints with a smile. I read Geoff Dyer novels purchased at Small World Books, observe the bodies at the famous outdoor weight-lifting gym just outside, watch surfers and skateboarders, try to empty myself out.

I try to avoid doing anything, until someone suggests that I contact one of the largest landowners in the area. "You can't understand Venice," they say, "without understanding Mona."

Mona lives on Electric Avenue, near Venice Boulevard. Stepping into Mona's house, I'm struck by one of the strangest sights I've ever seen. An array of seventeen televisions in the living room are all tuned to different channels, with the volume low but not all the way down—liberal commentators compete with conservatives competing with children's programming. I take the seat across from Mona, with my back to the screens.

Mona has spindly legs and long feet, wears pink pants, a dark-pink ballerina top, plastic sunglasses, and a blond wig. He says, "I'm not a girl, but I'm not a man either. I'm both. I think they both suck."

Mona says he's been here since 1969, but everybody seems to think he's been here longer. He started buying property in and around Venice in the sixties, back when his name was Roger. He owns more than forty properties, including office space on Windward Avenue, warehouses, and a fourteen-thousand-square-foot building he lived in for years.

When Google decided to open offices in Venice in 2010, it moved into a Frank Gehry building on Main. I pass it almost every day, with its famous sculpture of matte-black binoculars forty-five feet high pointing straight down into the sidewalk. For a company predicated on helping people find things, it's a bizarre choice, leasing a building framed by binoculars that can't see.

The binoculars building wasn't big enough for Google. It also wanted to rent one of Mona's properties, the old Gas Company Building, on the same block. Mona offered to rent the building to Google as long as he could keep his office there. Google balked. The search giant didn't want Mona in its Los Angeles headquarters. Mona told Google he'd just rent to someone else. Google executives learned that he was actually talking to other potential tenants, and now they rent Mona's building on Mona's terms.

It's the middle of the day. Mona drinks straight vodka without ice from a plastic cup. The house looks like a thrift store, but weirder. Racks of old clothing fill one room and spill into another. He talks fast, a stream of words that come so quickly, it can be hard to follow what he's saying.

He says, "Distraction is a good thing. It must have something to do with longevity and function. Everybody should just promote distraction at every level. I can't tell you, there has to be some risk. If you follow the course and logic of sensibility, I mean, right there you're sunk. You know what I mean?"

I have no idea what he means. I ask Mona about being a landlord in Venice. He says, "I'm not a landlord."

"You're not?"

"I'm not a Negro either. I'm not a cross-dresser and I'm not a transsexual and I'm not genderqueer. I don't want to be any of those things, and they're all abusive. Remember the word 'hippie'? It was a very pejorative word about unkempt people who didn't seem to take life seriously and were probably for whatever reason following some ideology that was pointless and would soon blow away."

"So 'landlord' is pejorative?"

"'Landlord' is boring, and don't say it again in my presence. I don't like it, so don't use it."

But Mona is a landlord with many properties and renters. He's also a developer with many employees. I wonder how anybody works for him. I find him incomprehensible. He's supposed to be the bridge between the old Venice—dropouts and surfers and freaks—and the new Venice of technological innovation. When I think of Mona as a bridge, all I can think of is the Tacoma Narrows Bridge, caught dramatically on film, its concrete and steel twisting, fluttering along its node in forty-mile-per-hour wind. And then I remember the lone scientist who knew that the wave oscillating the bridge had a stable point in the middle. And he knew he could walk safely out onto the bridge, which he did for a bit, returning before the structure collapsed into Puget Sound.

I can't bear to talk with Mona for more than half an hour, though later, when I listen to the tape, I find him surprisingly coherent and insightful and something of a poet.

"There is no history of Venice," Mona says. "Nor should there be. Everybody should shut up and stop talking about Venice. Everybody thinks they're clarifying something, when all they're doing is selling the hype."

4. THE SALESMAN

The TrueCar office is located at the corner of Broadway and Second in Santa Monica, on the northern end of Silicon Beach. TrueCar, a data-driven car-buying and -selling mobile marketplace, has outposts in San Francisco and Austin, but it has chosen to make this its headquarters, with a view of the ocean and the Santa Monica Pier. Large desks. Soft, balsa-wood-encased lighting.

I'm met by Neeraj Gunsagar, executive vice president and chief revenue officer. Gunsagar is responsible for growing revenue and all profit-driving functions. He's handsome and well dressed. We stroll past outdoor lounges and through a group of programmers, into his office, where we're joined by a public-relations person named Alan Ohnsman.

TrueCar went public in May 2014. Gunsagar explains, "There were 17.2 million new vehicles sold this year in America. There were 38 million used vehicles sold. The market is well over a trillion dollars."

Ohnsman sits slightly behind me on the right while Gunsagar explains that TrueCar is a CPA model. Cost per action. In other words, TrueCar gets paid by car dealers to introduce the dealers to buyers, but only if the dealers actually sell a car. He says we're moving away from the old Internet—cost per click—into a more exciting, target-specific environment. "There's no risk to dealers," he says. "TrueCar isn't focused on page views, it's not an advertising model; in fact, there's no advertising on the site."

"So what exactly is your article about?" Ohnsman asks.

I think about Shakespeare's murder on the boardwalk. The

other morning I jumped into the ocean. The water had been warming all summer and it felt perfect, but the tides were angry. It was early, and as I waded out, I looked toward the surfers up the coast in Santa Monica, framed by the Palisades. I felt the undertow slip its fingers around my ankles, pulling me under a wave and farther from shore. One moment the sand was beneath me, soft and silty, and then it was gone.

"I don't really know what it's about," I say. They nod thoughtfully.

"I was raised in Silicon Valley," Gunsagar says. "My father moved there in the sixties and was part of the initial, true Silicon Valley. I was born right next to Apple, in Saratoga. Silicon Valley has become a very efficient creator of technology enterprises, with all the venture capital right there and several generations of entrepreneurs. It's a well-balanced system. Compared to Silicon Valley, the Los Angeles tech scene is the Wild West."

We talk about Los Angeles. We talk about the heat. We talk about the changes in the neighborhood. The west side of Los Angeles is becoming a technology hub. Perhaps even the second largest in the United States. Perhaps the fifth largest in the world. "Why not?" Gunsagar asks. "L.A. has lots of great universities. Southern California has long been home to the aerospace industry. There's talent here," Gunsagar says. To him, Los Angeles is like a tree, the fruit hanging from its branches easily within reach. The question isn't, Why is technology moving to Los Angeles? but, rather, Why be anywhere else?

"People want to live in a city," Gunsagar says. "Los Angeles is a diverse city. If you go to a party in Los Angeles, you might meet an actress. But you might also meet someone who works in avionics, a manufacturer. San Francisco is a one-industry town. You don't meet anyone outside of the tech bubble, and that makes it hard to realize what real people want. They're making apps for themselves; in Los Angeles, companies are building technology people use. The Los Angeles metro area is as big as Mexico City."

Of course, Los Angeles is perhaps the most famous one-industry town in the world. The manufacturing sector has been obliterated. People in entertainment don't hang out with avionics engineers.

I mention the advent of self-driving cars. Gunsagar dismisses it with an easy smile, waving his hand as if he were sitting next to a smoker. "Most of these innovations are safety innovations. But cars aren't going anywhere. We're currently seeing the best car market we've ever seen. Ownership of a vehicle is the corner-stone of being an American.

"Do you own a car?" he asks.

"No," I say.

Gunsagar cocks his head before returning to his point. He gestures at the flotilla of engineers at their desks, crowding the expansive floor beyond his office. "I have a great team," he says. "A group of young guys who just kill themselves for this. To solve this one problem. Really smart people who love the challenge."

"The challenge of helping people buy a car?"

"A one-point-two-trillion-dollar auto market this year. There are millions of permutations of auto vehicles. Connecting these permutations to a consumer is an amazing challenge."

"So you're just helping people buy cars?"

5. THE FRIEND

Andrea[1] sits on the screened-in patio at a café on the northeast-ern edge of Santa Monica, where she lives. She's tall and olive-skinned, with short copper hair. When she sees me coming, she

---

1. Not her real name.

closes a mathematics textbook. She is considering going back to school to study economics. We're old friends, and it turns out that she had a relationship with Sris Sinnathamby, although they haven't been in touch in years.

"He helped pay for my school," Andrea says. "Sris has a lot of money. Like, he had multiple people to take care of his dog, even though he had a custody arrangement for the dog with his ex. He doted on his dog, but I didn't like how he treated other people. He always wanted employees to make exceptions for him." Andrea thinks Sinnathamby was classist. She says she stopped seeing him because his worldview made her uncomfortable.

The night Shakespeare was killed, after Guzman took off, the homeless who had been celebrating with Shakespeare attacked Sinnathamby. Derick Noralez, whom everyone called Bigz, threw Sinnathamby to the ground. A disabled man beat Sinnathamby over the head with the footrest of his wheelchair. They beat him so badly that he ended up in the hospital with a broken collarbone and eye socket. At the hospital they put twenty-four staples in his head.

Multiple witnesses told the police they heard Sinnathamby telling Guzman, "Kill that nigger." But if you watch the surveillance tape, the witnesses' account of Sinnathamby instructing Guzman to kill Shakespeare is hard to believe. The witnesses are fifteen feet away, at least, and Guzman is on one side of Sinnathamby, with Shakespeare on the other. He doesn't appear to be yelling, so even if Sinnathamby said something, it seems unlikely the witnesses would have heard it.

The police finally arrived on the scene more than half an hour later. They arrested Sinnathamby on murder charges before taking him to the hospital. His bail was set at $1 million, which he posted. His passport was confiscated, and he had to wear an ankle bracelet. The men who beat Sinnathamby weren't charged.

The merchants along the boardwalk say Sinnathamby is part

of the community, that he knows how to get along with the homeless like any boardwalk merchant has to. The homeless are a part of the place. When a neighborhood coalition suggested hiring private security for the area several years ago, Sinnathamby organized a meeting at his hotel and argued against the idea.

Andrea insists that Sinnathamby despised the homeless. "He took me out for dinner one night. We walked past a giant construction site that took up the entire block. He spread his arms and bragged, 'All of this belongs to me.'"

"What about the homeless?" she asked.

"They have to go," he replied.

Sinnathamby's lawyer, Alan Jackson, declined my requests for an interview with Sinnathamby, but he says that his client doesn't own anything fitting the description of an entire block. Andrea, for her part, told the story to multiple people at the time.

After meeting Andrea, I re-watch the video from the night of Shakespeare's murder. There's Sinnathamby talking with someone carrying a sleeping bag. Then Guzman strolls into the center of the screen, wearing basketball shorts with his hands clasped behind his back. Sinnathamby moves toward the right of the frame, where he's speaking with someone off camera. Guzman follows, casually pulls a gun from his shorts pocket, and fires four shots toward the water.

Fifteen seconds later, Shakespeare and Sinnathamby reenter the frame. Shakespeare is agitated, pointing at Guzman, who is still holding the gun. Sinnathamby positions himself between the two men, doing everything he can to keep them apart. It looks like Sinnathamby is alternately trying to hold Shakespeare back and get Guzman to lower the gun. At one point, Sinnathamby approaches Guzman with his arms out, as if to give him a hug. But Shakespeare follows, and Sinnathamby turns to push Shakespeare back.

Suddenly, Guzman closes the distance between them. Then

Shakespeare gets around Sinnathamby and leaps toward Guzman. Guzman sidesteps, firing multiple shots at Shakespeare at close range.

Guzman leaves, gesturing for Sinnathamby to follow, but he stays.

Sinnathamby is possibly the hero of this complicated story.

6. THE DEALER

Danny Zappin arrived in Los Angeles in 2004 after spending two years in the federal penitentiary in Lompoc. He had four months left on his sentence—he'd been convicted of smuggling ecstasy—and the court agreed to let him serve them under house arrest at his friend Paul's place, on Martel near the corner of Sunset and La Brea in Hollywood.

It was a rough part of town in 2004, but Danny didn't get to see much of it. He was allowed out of Paul's house only for his drug tests and to work as a valet in Beverly Hills. Before going to prison, he was an aspiring actor and filmmaker. He'd been to film school in South Florida in the nineties and shot music videos for college bands using his Canon XL1, one of the first affordable high-end digital video cameras.

The view from the window at Paul's place was of a city without seasons. Danny could see the streets that had always lured would-be stars and starlets, but he was forbidden from interacting with them. Danny wanted to be a star, but he was a convicted felon lacking connections. He'd shot hundreds of hours of footage: film shorts, music videos, random tape. But he had no way to get it seen or distributed. Before he'd gone to prison, he would show videos to friends; he'd even been in a few small festivals.

In 2005, still under house arrest, Danny got his first email address. He began to create a social life for himself online. He found MySpace, the website people thought might connect the content in Los Angeles with the technology of Silicon Valley. And maybe it did, because MySpace led Danny Zappin to YouTube, which became an obsession.

YouTube was just months old when Danny started uploading music videos and clips from his director's reel. He re-edited and mashed some of it together. The response was overwhelming. YouTube was growing fast but was lacking original content. Viewers left comments telling him what they wanted. He wrote comments back that were playful, funny. He made a video of himself goofy-dancing, challenging his fans to dance worse. There were hundreds of comments. He called himself Danny Diamond. His YouTube channel was called the Diamond Factory. Danny had always wanted to break into Hollywood, but on YouTube, unlike in Hollywood, you didn't have to audition. It was exhilarating to have access to a global audience and upload stuff and just see the number of views explode. You could build a following and lots of subscribers, distribute work directly to a wildly enthusiastic audience of your own creation.

As his mandatory home confinement ended, Hollywood still seemed out of reach, but that didn't matter anymore. He'd left Hollywood behind without leaving his room.

Now I'm sitting across from Danny, under a gigantic peaked skylight, in a conference room that used to be an art gallery. He has short red hair and the calculating calm of a surfer. Twelve large paintings hang high on the walls above us, including an orange portrait of Frida Kahlo; a sharp blue graphic that looks like strands of fiber stabbing themselves, and a similar painting in gray; and two colorful squares by the spray-paint artist Ricky Watts.

"I was a power user in the early days," Danny says. "I knew how to tag, title, get on a list, engage the audience through comments. I was obsessed and excited about creating content and music videos."

Soon after he completed his sentence, he moved in with his girlfriend, Lisa Donovan, in Venice. Venice was more Danny's style.

Venice was for outsiders, for people who made things. Danny was an actor and filmmaker, but he had no access. For him, and many before him, serious artists didn't stand in front of a Hollywood studio waiting to be let in. They went to Venice instead.

Danny arrived in 2005. "Venice was much edgier in those days and had not been gentrified," Danny says. "Police helicopters were constantly flying over my neighborhood. Gang violence was still a big issue. There was no Silicon Beach or any tech scene to speak of. I liked the grittiness and artistic edge. It felt more real than Hollywood, and I found the people to be far more interesting."

Lisa and Danny started making videos together, and Lisa's channel exploded. What Danny and Lisa wanted wasn't really any different from what more-mainstream performers want: validation, access, power. And then an idea occurred to them. Couldn't they team up with other YouTube power users?

"We got to know all these people from different parts of the country, and some of them came to Venice to visit, and it became clear that to do this well, you sort of needed some infrastructure," Danny says. "It didn't make sense to have every person working for themselves and maintaining all the costs of their own channel. So we came up with the idea of creating something like a studio to help people create content and integrate operations and bring in brand deals and everything."

They lived in an apartment just off Abbot Kinney Boulevard. Other YouTube performers started arriving in Venice to work with the nascent studio, which they dubbed Maker. "We had a lot of the top stars at the time, and they all worked together blowing up new people like Kassem G and Shay Carl, HiimRawn and Pete and Epic Rap Battles, Nice Peter," Danny says. "And by getting these people with a half a million subscribers to recommend new talent and collaborate, we created the biggest, fastest-growing channels."

Maker was the first huge YouTube success. To keep growing quickly, it accepted venture capital. But the investors decided they didn't want Danny as CEO, citing his felony conviction. Fights erupted between the studio and the talent, most noticeably with Ray William Johnson, possibly Maker's biggest star, who accused Maker of trying to strong-arm him into signing away the rights to shows he created prior to joining the studio.

Ultimately Danny got pushed out, or, depending on who's telling the story, he resigned. Lawsuits are still pending. He split up with Lisa. Maker was sold to Disney for half a billion dollars. Danny walked away with a reported $25 million.

Now Danny owns Zealot Networks. Its offices are across Venice Boulevard, a short walk from where Mona lives. Danny lives in a nice house on one of the neighborhood's remaining canals. When the city tried to fill in all the canals after annexing Venice in 1925, there wasn't enough of a tax base to pay for the work. Ironically, the remaining canals are now among the most desirable places to live in Venice.

Zealot bought eighteen media companies in its first year. The onetime felon, who gleefully made dancing videos to share with his fans, is now looking for a bigger piece of the pie. You're only an outsider for so long.

7. THE GUN FOR HIRE

I drive south from Venice, past the marina. Past Playa Vista, where shining skeletons of the new Facebook offices are rising from the marsh, under the planes thunderously approaching LAX, then heading on to El Segundo. I'm not sure what I'm hoping to find. I feel like some kind of holistic detective, sifting through evidence, trying to piece something together without knowing the crime I'm trying to solve.

Some people think El Segundo is part of Silicon Beach, though it seems awfully far away. Borders are not always so easy to define until you cross one. All I know is that El Segundo was established as Standard Oil's second refinery on the West Coast. Now it's a warren of eight-lane boulevards and faceless office parks, pressed between the ocean and hills covered with slowly swinging derricks.

I park at a monstrous cube of glass—one of a dozen that stand near each other like a see-through fort—and take the elevator to the eighth floor to meet Chuck Davis, the CEO of Swagbucks. Swagbucks offers rewards to people who buy things online. Previously Chuck led Disney's online business group. He says Swagbucks had no trouble hiring talent in Los Angeles. "The bigger problem was the investors," he says. "They were all up north. They wanted us to be in Silicon Valley."

Chuck's helped Disney Internet Group with online shopping and travel, sales and subscriptions. "The word 'e-commerce' didn't exist yet," he says. Then Chuck moved over to Shopzilla, which was sold to Scripps. After that he joined Fandango, which had been operating in the same building. He left one rapidly expanding company for another. Fandango was sold to Comcast, and Chuck stayed on board until a few months after Comcast acquired NBCUniversal. "I believe as CEOs we rent our roles," Chuck says. "We're here to do an assignment: create value for the investors."

It makes me think of a baseball player casually approaching home plate, thinking about getting back to his family, ready for the game to be over. Or any time our passion leaves us. *We rent our roles.*

It reminds me of a woman I was in love with. It wasn't too long ago. She was living with one of her clients, but he was out of town for a few days. He was worth hundreds of millions of dollars. They lived in a mansion and had a view of the Golden Gate Bridge that looked like a picture sold to tourists. She had long arms and legs and moved with uncanny grace. Men had ghostwritten memoirs for her, signed over apartment complexes, cowritten her dissertation. In the mansion, there were two boxes of drugs, carefully organized and labeled: *Ketamine, Cocaine, Moon Rocks*. There was a new Tesla parked in the garage. And I remember we took acid and sat on a bench down the street from the mansion. And I realized, through the haze of drugs and desire, that no matter how long I stayed, ultimately I would have to leave—that I wasn't jealous of the men she loved for free; I was jealous of the men who could afford her.

8. THE GENIUS

Meredith Perry just turned twenty-six. Her company is called uBeam, which is developing a device to make electricity wireless. Not like those pads you put your phone on for charging; more like Wi-Fi for electricity. *Power. Always. Anywhere*, the uBeam website promises. In 2014, Mark Cuban, Marissa Mayer, and Andreessen Horowitz, among others, invested $10 million in Meredith's company.

What's interesting to me about uBeam is that it will be a new technology—if it works. Other start-ups, like TrueCar, are just creating digital versions of services that have been around for decades—lead generators, coupons, catalogs. But sending electricity through the air is something scientists and engineers have been trying to crack since Tesla (Nikola, not Elon).

The uBeam headquarters are on Main Street in Santa Monica, less than a mile from TrueCar. The doors are thick steel, the kind you'd see at a bank or an intelligence agency. The office has three labs, a machine shop, and a wall of glass enclosing a work area.

There is an air of secrecy and a lack of windows. I'm not allowed to take pictures.

A publicist ushers me down the narrow hallway, back to meet Meredith. We pass a variety of mostly empty rooms. For a hot company with tons of funding, it's surprisingly underpopulated. In the hallway there are a handful of employees tapping on laptops at a long table, but most of the spaces are empty.

Meredith greets me, and we sit at a table in her office. I sit cross-legged on the couch, and she sits in a chair. In her sweater, sneakers, and jeans, she looks and sounds like a college student: smart, young, and overflowing with enthusiasm. She starts by trying to explain what an ultrasonic transducer is. Effectively a little transmitter, like the ones used in sonar detection. Her transducer creates a high-frequency sound wave, which a receiver converts into electricity. She says that the receiver could be packaged into something like a cell phone case.

Meredith tells me, "I think the reason I can tackle complex technology is because I'm good at breaking down complex problems and explaining them to other people."

I nod, but I still don't actually understand how an ultrasonic transducer works.

"My approach has always been top down," Perry says. "I get interested in crazy complex scientific problems, then I learn everything I need to know in order to solve them. Part of that is ADD. I don't want to have to go to four years of electrical-engineering school." People in Venice often talk about ADD.

Perry grew up in Princeton, New Jersey. Her father is a plastic surgeon who, she says, developed the world's best skin creams. Her mother was a child psychologist. "My brother is a comedy writer named Penis Bailey," she says. "He's going to be famous. And my sister is a private investigator."

"What's your brother's name?" I ask.

"Penis Bailey," she repeats.

"As a kid, I was curious," she continues. "I asked a zillion questions. I was that annoying person where, anything you said, I'd be like, 'But wait! Why? Tell me how that works!' And my father just kept answering. He always had the answers."

Meredith takes a bag down from the shelf near her desk. "I have, like, a zillion little colored notebooks with all my inventions. My grandpa and I used to write letters back and forth on invention ideas."

She takes out a notebook. She says she filled them with ideas while she was in college, at the University of Pennsylvania, where she studied astrobiology. The notebooks detail inventions like a jacket that's also an air bag, for people riding motorcycles. Or a tactile gaming vest, so if you were playing a video game and somebody punched your avatar, you could feel the punch in your own chest. There are designs for an umbrella to use while riding a bicycle and a touch-simulation back massager.

Like so many other founders I've met here, she says she chose Southern California over Silicon Valley for the quality of life. All the tech people in L.A. seem to be in agreement on the high standard of living and cheap rent.

"Los Angeles is a city of entrepreneurs," Perry says. "Here you form a production company and you pitch your movie to a producer and that's your project. There's a lot of entrepreneurial DNA in this town. It's an inspiring place to be." She's twenty-six years old and she's lived here a year and now she's explaining the city's sociology to me. People say she's a genius, but what does that even mean? I was at a party at Sundance once with James Franco's manager and his wife. His wife introduced me to someone as a genius. Then she introduced me to ten more filmmakers and writers, all geniuses as well. If there is one place where being a genius means nothing, it's Los Angeles.

.   .   .

A number of scientists have attacked Perry's invention. The skeptics say that generating sufficient power with uBeam's technology would likely make people nearby nauseous and cause hearing loss. By May 2015, none of the scientists listed on uBeam's patents other than Perry were still at the company. The CTO and CFO had both left, and in April a former VP of engineering wrote a series of blog posts calling the fundamental technology "not even remotely practical."

I reread the transcripts of my recorded conversation with Meredith. I come across something she said when we were talking about her brother. The one who goes by Penis Bailey and is embarking on a career as a comedy rap musician with lyrics like "You couldn't see me coaching Little League / Rather get my pickle squeezed by a chick with triple-Ds." He wears a silver necklace with a jewel-encrusted pendant in the shape of a large penis. In an interview, he said his penis pendant is always hard because he's always hard.

"My brother just moved to L.A.," Meredith told me. "He's going to be LA's next biggest movie star. I guarantee you. I brought him over to Warner Bros., and within five minutes the head of feature films asked him to do punch-ups for all their scripts."

"How did you bring him over to Warner?" I asked. She said she'd given a talk there on technology. That part made sense. Meredith is a tech celebrity. Everyone in the L.A. tech scene has heard of her, and Los Angeles is a town obsessed with celebrity. But the idea that a Hollywood executive would meet a kid with sunglasses and a hoodie wearing a large penis necklace and immediately give him scripts to rewrite was beyond belief. A lot of people—who are not wearing penis necklaces—meet studio executives by chance, and none of them are charged with revising the studio's entire slate.

Reading through my conversation with Meredith, I'm struck by an absurd optimism, a pathological confidence that's brought people west for more than a hundred years, first for gold, then for fame. Maybe that's why Silicon Beach landed here in Los Angeles, where the motto has always been "Fake it till you make it."

9. THE HEADSET

Most of the founders I talk to are less social than Meredith. They're not antisocial, but when I ask what they do outside of work, they tilt their heads, as if I were trying to trick them.

"It's essential to move as fast as possible," says Alex Rosenfeld, the founder and CEO of Vrideo, a virtual reality company working out of ROC, which describes itself as "a collaborative workspace for start-ups, entrepreneurs, and small businesses in the heart of Silicon Beach." Vrideo's goal is to be the Vimeo or YouTube of VR. "Every day or week or month advantage we build in right now will be the equivalent of a year or two years' advantage in three years' time," Alex says. "If that makes any sense."

"Sure," I say. Though I'm not sure it does. Friendster had a big advantage over Facebook, and where are they now?

Virtual reality is the great metaphor of our time. All the self-help business books talk about willing yourself to success, creating your own reality. A virtual reality start-up is like a company trying to create its own reality by creating its own reality. "One of the cool things we've been involved in this past year is launching the first-ever virtual reality film festival," Alex says. "We did a ten-city tour across North America with thirty filmmakers and crowds of around four hundred people for each event."

I stop Alex because I want to understand something. "So you had four hundred people in a room wearing headsets, all watching their own virtual reality movie."

"That's right."

"If they're watching it on headsets, couldn't they just watch it from anywhere? Why do they even need to be in the same place?"

"Very few people have the headsets right now," Alex says by way of explanation.

A room with four hundred people, all exploring their own worlds inside their headsets and headphones, unable to see or hear one another, potentially unaware of one another's existence. "You call that bringing people together?" I ask.

10. THE DOMINATRIX

A friend tells me that a Los Angeles dominatrix named Ms. Edie Elson will have interesting things to say about Silicon Beach. I contact Ms. Elson and tell her I would like to talk to her about how all the new tech companies have affected her business.

Ms. Elson invites me to come over the next morning. She gives me the code to her building and tells me to be at her door at exactly 10:20 a.m. Just before I arrive in front of the large steel door, Ms. Elson texts and instructs me to "take two steps inside after you open the door and do not turn around."

I consider knocking but instead push the heavy door open, as I was told, and take two steps into the dark.

"Turn to your right. I want to look at you," a voice behind me says. The voice is calm, with an aristocratic edge.

I turn, but I can't see anything. I feel her hands on my shoulder, tracing down my body, over my ribs, then onto my upper thighs, then working their way inside my shirt, her sharp nails circling my nipples. It feels as if she's memorizing me with her fingers. I've written about my sexual proclivities and experience with BDSM. One of my books is called *My Girlfriend Comes to the City and Beats Me Up.* Yet I feel certain I'm a complete stranger to her. All she knows is that I'm a journalist here to interview her about Silicon Beach.

I follow her into the sitting room. She sprawls across a large maroon leather chair. She's wearing a short silk robe, sheer tan stockings with a seam up the back, short cream-colored heels.

She points to the footstool in front of her, and I take a seat at her feet.

"Could you imagine what it would be like to live here as my slave?" she asks.

I could. She looks like Rita Hayworth and speaks as if she were clasping an unlit cigarette in a long holder. She explains that I would pay all the rent and make breakfast for her in the mornings. "Just for a month or two," she says. "A break from your everyday life."

She shows me the slave's quarters. Essentially a janitor's closet large enough for a small bed. She's had bars installed on the outside of the window. I wonder if this is how the poorer residents feel around Venice Beach, like they're paying full rent but living in a closet and doing all the work while other people make all the money. Of course, it's different when it's between consenting adults. I imagine life in the janitor's closet. Locked inside, lying on the small bed, riven with desire.

The walls of the janitor's closet aren't quite high enough to reach the ceiling. "I'd like to put barbed wire along the top so you can't climb out. Are you handy?" Ms. Elson asks.

"Not really," I reply.

She moves close and whispers in my ear, "I know what you need."

She assures me she'd give me enough time to write if I moved into the slave's quarters. She knows I would still need to do my work; how else could I pay the rent? She leads me around the rest of the space. Shows me the bathroom, the second room, with a collection of toys: metal chastity devices, leather hoods, bondage bags. I smile enigmatically. I know I'm not going to move in with her, though I find it tempting. I've tried to live in a fantasy before, even succeeded for a time. But it's not sustainable. Then again, what is?

I'm amazed that even at forty-three, life is still completely unpredictable. Strange and magical things can still happen. It's never too late to figure out who you are, then change your mind.

BDSM is a fantasy involving power, but it mirrors real life, with leaders and followers, creators and fans, parents and children. One group, dominants, or tops, exerts control over another, submissives or bottoms or slaves. And sometimes the dominant person wants to give up control and sometimes they don't. Sometimes the fantasy involves fighting back and losing. When you're in bondage, tightly bound, layered in rope, perhaps hooded and gagged, you're not responsible for anything. It's inherently unequal yet often very loving. The world of BDSM is almost obsessively safe. Everything is negotiated in advance. People are checked in on. It's the exact opposite of the real world, where the powerful and the powerless smash against each other like opposing storm fronts.

11. THE MARINE

Paige Craig, a former marine turned venture capitalist, wants to go for a hike in Runyon Canyon. It's ten a.m. I don't mind hiking, but I'm not one of those people who would put *Loves hiking* in my dating profile.

"He's just like the dominatrix," my editor tells me. "He's forcing you to do something you don't want to do." Editors always want to make a link between everything. But real life is harder to pin down. Maybe the clearer link is to Danny Zappin. Craig moved into Danny's old house near Abbot Kinney Boulevard and still gets his mail.

Craig, who runs a fund investing in nascent Los Angeles technology companies, coined the term "Silicon Beach." He thought it would help bring founders to the area. He wasn't exactly born into the investor class. He spent his early childhood in Seattle, where his family lived above a Chinese egg market. Then they lived in Pittsburgh. And then Idaho, where his dad worked in a lead factory. Then they made their way to Los Angeles. For a long time, he says, his bed was the backseat of the family car. "In high school I did football, I wrestled a little bit, I was on the science and math league teams. I was driven. I had this intensity. I ended up getting recruited by West Point," he says. "I loved it at first. And then realized I'm a bad fit for traditional military. I'm not very good at listening to what other people tell me to do."

Craig dropped out of West Point after his third year and began cruising around the country, living out of his car. In New York City he saw a Marine Corps recruiting ad. "I drove down to the local office. And of course the Marine Corps accepts everyone, so I was in."

My brother was rejected by the Marines, so I'm pretty sure Paige's statement isn't accurate. But maybe it seems that way to him. My brother is a police officer in Chicago now, the murder capital of America. He patrols the area on the South Side known as Chi-Raq, a beat cop with blond hair and a Chicago flag stitched on his sleeve in the most segregated city in the country.

Craig stops walking and unscrews his water bottle. I unscrew the water bottle he gave me. I've been following just behind, holding my phone near his face to record him as he talks. It's sunny, and I wish I'd worn a hat. We've been walking for a while, but there are still trees, and it feels like we're a long way from the top. We look at each other for a moment. "Are you getting what you need?" Craig asks.

"I hope so," I say, digging my inhaler out of my backpack.

"Are you all right?" he asks.

"I'm in great shape," I tell him, and we continue.

After five years in the Marine Corps, Paige left the service and went to work as a military contractor in Northern Virginia. "And then, when the war in Iraq started, I was like, I want to go there. This is the culmination of all my training. I want to be in the middle of it."

Paige flew into Jordan, found a taxi driver to take him into Baghdad for $200, and set up shop with ten grand that he carried in camera bags. This was post-invasion, roughly October of 2003. "My pitch was 'I will do anything.' Imagine, like, a TaskRabbit for Iraq. When you need shit done, we get it done. I got paid to move trash out of al-Anbar. We got paid to deal with scrapped weaponry up and down the highway to Basra, which is all the tanks and all the shit we destroyed and blew up—getting rid of all that shit."

In other words, somehow he went from doing odd jobs to doing bigger odd jobs, like taking care of destroyed tanks on the highways. Paige is reluctant to get into the specifics. He says, "The kind of work we did, I can't get into."

The things Paige can't get into are psychological operation missions, or psyops. In 2005, the *Los Angeles Times* revealed that Paige's company, the Lincoln Group, used its network of connections to plant slanted news stories written by the Defense Department in foreign publications, often by paying the editors of those publications. Also in 2005, the *New York Times* reported that the Lincoln Group had become the main civilian contractor for an aggressive propaganda campaign in Anbar Province, the Sunni stronghold where al-Qaeda in Iraq took root. (Nine years later, al-Qaeda in Iraq would become what we know as ISIS.) The *Times* article pointed out that much of Paige's company's marketing materials at the time contained untruths, like listing partners who hadn't actually done work with the company or claiming affiliations with other, larger companies, like Omnicom, that it hadn't actually worked with.

In less than two years, the Lincoln Group had grown into a propaganda juggernaut, with more than $100 million in military contracts. The war in Iraq made Paige rich.

"I realized in my fifth year that if I kept going, I was either going to be that dude who is dead in some war zone, or I was going to end up a very lonely rich dude who does not enjoy life. I sold the business."

From Iraq, Paige went off to Egypt and Puerto Rico, Australia, D.C., L.A., Boston, and Boulder. He thought of doing microfinance in countries like Sudan. Then he ended up in San Francisco and went to TechCrunch50, a conference started by a popular blog where fledgling start-ups compete for a $50,000 prize. "I was like, Holy shit, this is how the Googles of the world get created?" he says.

We reach the top of the mountain. The view is outrageous, and I'm exhausted. Two helicopters are circling nearby. A woman has hurt herself down the trail. One helicopter approaches, hovering just above her. A man slides down a rope, lands on the ground, and unhitches. Craig wants to watch the scene unfold, but I feel like I'm dying under the California sun and ask if we can head down the mountain.

As we approach the base of the canyon, I can see a public park full of families with their children and pets, blankets spread between the trail and the parking lots. "What you have to be willing to give up to be successful in a start-up is extreme. You wake up and you're putting everything—your time, your relationships, every dollar, every asset you ever earned—it's all going to this one thing, and you know every day that it's fragile and can be destroyed at any moment. A bad contract, poor execution, a bad story—so many things could kill your business. And you're asking yourself, Why the fuck am I doing this? What's the meaning of all this?"

Craig talked a lot about the importance of stories for a start-up, and the ability to communicate your story, first to investors and then to customers. Joan Didion didn't live far from here when she wrote her elegy to the late sixties in Los Angeles, *The White Album*. It begins, "We tell ourselves stories in order to live." But she was talking about a time when she had stopped believing those stories. The acid wasn't doing what it was supposed to. The speed freaks were taking over. The movement was turning murderous.

They called it the Age of Aquarius. Manson called it Helter Skelter. Silicon Beach is a catchphrase meant to convey a story. Something more than surfers and money and drugs. But silicon is just sand.

12. THE PRINCE

Tao Ruspoli is an actual Italian prince. He lives in a small house near Abbot Kinney Boulevard, in the heart of Venice, equidistant from the canals, the ocean, and Santa Monica. The house is only eight hundred square feet, with one bedroom, but there's extra land where he's parked four vintage trailers. He's also built an outdoor bathroom and an outdoor office surrounded by glass, like an oversize phone booth.

Ruspoli had met Mona fifteen years before. He was living in a house in Coldwater Canyon that he was supposed to inherit from his father. "My dad sold our family castle to get us this little house. Then my mom married an art forger who ended up going to prison in Spain, and I ended up with all these lawsuits. My friend David Greenberg said, 'You've got to call my friend Mona.' He didn't dress as a woman then, but he had these nine-inch-long fingernails." Mona knew about real estate and advised Ruspoli on his lawsuits in Coldwater. "He really knew what he was talking about," Ruspoli says, "but in the end we lost the house."

After that he moved into a school bus he'd bought on eBay. In 2001, he took the bus to Burning Man. Mona moved in with him there, out in the desert. "We lived out there on the bus for, like, eight months, shooting video. When we came back, Mona let me park in the Gas Company lot."

I clarify that we're talking about the building where Google is now, a mile away from Paige Craig's place. "Yes," he says. "The Google building." This was years before Google started renting the offices, asking potential hires if they "prefer the sand and surf over a mountain view? Want three hundred days of sun a year?" And promising "a climbing wall, an outdoor movie theater, a rooftop deck with views of Venice Beach, and a Michael Mina–trained chef."

Ruspoli decided to start a filmmaking collective, which he ran out of the bus. "It was funny because I was obviously living there. I would joke that it had all the luxuries and none of the essentials. It had editing systems and nice couches but no bathroom, no shower, no kitchen. I used the bathrooms and shower in the Gas Company Building."

While living in the bus and running the filmmaking collective, Ruspoli made a number of well-regarded documentaries on topics as varied as flamenco and his family's drug addictions.

In 2002, he met a girl who had come to L.A. to pursue an acting career, and they fell in love. She was eighteen; Ruspoli was twenty-six. She moved into the bus with him, which is where they were married. The actress's name is Olivia Wilde. They lived in the parking lot, but the editing equipment was now in an office building, so there was more room in the bus. "We were married for eight years. We drove the bus across the country to New York, where Olivia was doing a TV show. By the time I got back to Venice, six months later, everything had changed. It was like Beverly Hills. And I was part of that too, in a way. I was living this kind of fancy life with Olivia and everything. But we still wanted to be in Venice."

In 2008, Ruspoli's first narrative feature, *Fix*, starring Olivia

Wilde, premiered in competition at Slamdance, the film festival set up in shaggy opposition to Sundance. Slamdance is an outsider festival, and yet it has become a very prestigious place to premiere. It's for the insiders among the outsiders, which would be an interesting way to describe Ruspoli, who has always been at the center of something on the periphery.

He shows me a coffee table book full of his photographs. He is an excellent photographer. Pictures of the bus on Abbot Kinney and at Burning Man. The boardwalk in 2005. The desert images emit a sense of stark freedom with wide landscapes, but on closer inspection they seem to suggest a giant, colorful parade.

Olivia Wilde and Tao separated in 2011. It might seem like she left the beach for Hollywood, but Tao thinks eight years is a successful marriage. I was engaged in my early twenties to a woman I was with for two and a half years, and I've often wished we had gone through with the marriage, even with the inevitable divorce. Just because something doesn't last forever doesn't make it a failure.

13. I'M STILL HERE

On October 9, 2015, Francisco Cardenaz Guzman, the man accused of shooting Shakespeare, was finally found and arrested by the LAPD fugitive task force. He's being held on $3 million bail. The biggest question hanging over the case for me is how it came to be that Sinnathamby, a rich property owner, was in a vehicle driven by Guzman, a known gang member. Alan Jackson, Sinnathamby's lawyer, says Sinnathamby and Guzman met at a bar earlier that night and didn't previously know each other.

According to Jackson, Sinnathamby was at the bar with his ex-girlfriend and another friend. The area was very busy that night, and Sinnathamby was unable to hail a cab. Guzman offered

Sinnathamby and the women a lift. "It's not unusual to accept a ride from a stranger in Venice," Jackson says. "That's the culture of the beach."

Is it, though? A gang member and a real estate baron seem like an unusual combination. All I know for certain is what's in the video: a man who appears to be Guzman shooting Shakespeare three times, the homeless grabbing and beating Sinnathamby after Guzman runs away.

Today everything seems peaceful by the Cadillac Hotel. It's early in the morning, and I'm up, wandering the beach. I like it most here at dawn, when there's still a soft purple bruise on the edge of the horizon. I'm struck with a strong urge to stay, though I live on the other side of the country, in New York. At the same time, I've lived lots of places. I'm open to change. I'm the most inconsistent person I know.

Two weeks after Guzman's arrest, a man on a bicycle identified by the police as fifty-five-year-old Edward Martinez spit on the picture of Shakespeare at the makeshift boardwalk memorial. Martinez turned to the homeless men nearby and said, according to witnesses, "You guys are next." Derick Noralez, one of Sris Sinnathamby's alleged attackers the night of the killing, clotheslined Martinez. Several of the other homeless joined in, and Martinez ended up being hospitalized for head injuries. They were convicted of assault with a deadly weapon, the weapon being the footrest of the wheelchair of one of the homeless residents.

In the surveillance video on the night of Shakespeare's murder, a man can be seen beating Sinnathamby with the footrest of a wheelchair.

Most of the witnesses who remember Sinnathamby telling Guzman to "kill that nigger" have now spent time in jail themselves. (Guzman's lawyer, Garrett Zelen, won't concede that the figure in the video is his client. Guzman has pleaded not guilty to the charges.) At least one of the witnesses has speculated that the confrontation with Martinez could have been a setup to discredit them, according to the *Argonaut*, a free Venice newspaper. In court briefings, the prosecutors seem to agree, intimating that Martinez was acting on behalf of the Venice 13, Guzman's gang.

Ultimately, the case against Sinnathamby is dismissed for lack of evidence. "There's going to be some work required to get his good name back," Jackson says. "But he's looking forward to being an integral part of the Venice community again." Jackson says he's planning to file a motion to have Sinnathamby declared innocent.

Shakespeare's memorial is still standing, the picture surrounded by candles and totems. I pass it before walking across the quarter-mile expanse of sand to the ocean.

The water is much colder than when I first arrived and shocks me awake. I dive in—thinking of dead poets, third-round funding, seed funding, pre–seed funding, series A—and emerge into the soft haze of a mild and cloudy day, thirty, forty feet from shore. The sun is hidden and the color drained from the sky. Stores are slowly opening on the boardwalk, shop owners rattling and raising the steel gates. Artists are setting up tables to sell pictures at the edge of the beach. I wonder, Is this just a dream? Or is it the American dream?

Many of the homeless are still sleeping; I can see the dark outlines of their bags as well as a house painted white and blue and named for a smartphone app. I swim back toward shore. I've always wanted to settle down, but I never did. I wrote in an essay, applying to law school, "I left home when I was thirteen. It was the best decision I ever made." I was accepted to the University of Virginia, but I decided not to go. I was homeless the entire year I was in eighth grade, until the beginning of high school, and I never really stopped being a runaway. I never did go home. I'm driven but restless. I want to achieve, but I don't know what. I have so much ambition, like Venice, like Abbot Kinney building canals in a marsh nobody wanted. Seeing the possible in the impossible. Though when it didn't work out quite as planned, Kinney—like Paige Craig, like Danny Zappin—made the best of the situation. They took what they saw with both hands, grabbing as much ocean and land as they could.

—Los Angeles, 2015

Acknowledgments

I'd like to thank Ethan Nosowsky—an editor is not an easy person to find—and everyone at Graywolf Press.

Stephen Elliott is the author of eight books, including *The Adderall Diaries*, a best book of the year in *Time Out New York*, a best book of 2009 in *Kirkus Reviews*, and one of fifty notable books in the *San Francisco Chronicle*.

His novel *Happy Baby* was a finalist for the New York Public Library's Young Lions Award as well as a best book of the year in *Salon.com*, *Newsday*, *Newcity*, the *Journal News*, and the *Village Voice*.

Elliott's writing has been featured in *Esquire*, the *New York Times*, the *Believer*, *GQ*, *Best American Non-Required Reading*, *Best American Erotica*, and *Best Sex Writing*.

He is the founding editor of the *Rumpus* and senior editor at *Epic Magazine*. He created the web series *Driven* and has directed three movies: *About Cherry*, *Happy Baby*, and *After Adderall*.

The text of *Sometimes I Think About It* is set in Utopia. Book design and composition by Bookmobile Design and Digital Publisher Services, Minneapolis, Minnesota. Manufactured by Versa Press on acid-free, 30 percent postconsumer wastepaper.